MEIN KAMPF:
A Translation Controversy

MEIN KAMPF:

A Translation Controversy

An Analysis, Critique, and Revelation

Mein Kampf *has been controversial for many reasons. One of the greatest controversies has been over the English translations. We will analyze the various English translations and identify problems, mistranslations, inaccurate translations, and outright embellishment. From this we will then determine which translation is the most true to the original German version of* Mein Kampf *and discover previously unknown aspects of* Mein Kampf.

Analysis by Michael Ford

Elite Minds Inc., PUBLISHER

An Analysis of MEIN KAMPF

BY ADOLF HITLER

A CRITICAL ANALYSIS OF PAST ENGLISH TRANSLATIONS

Mein Kampf: A Translation Controversy, Second Edition
© Copyright 2009 Elite Minds Inc. All Rights Reserved.

Quotes are copyrighted by their respective rights owners. This work is a commentary and criticism and is intended to be a scholarly criticism for educational purposes. The included quotes are used under fair-use Section 107 as defined by the U.S. Copyright Office.

For permission to quote from this book, contact the publisher at support@EliteMindsInc.com

CONTENTS

Introduction Page	7
Understanding Mein Kampf	12
Known Translations	22
The Ford Translation	29
Hitlerisms	32
German Race References Explained	35
Words and Grammar	39
Errors in Mein Kampf	43
Conclusion	44
Appendix A - Errors Documented In Detail	46
Appendix B - Völkischer Beobachter	196

Listen To Mein Kampf

The Only English Translation Available In Audio
It Is Easy To Listen

Now you can listen to *Mein Kampf* in your car, on your MP3 player, or with your computer. This is the full, uncensored Ford Translation. Audio includes many extras and bonus material not available in the printed book. Listen again after you finish reading the book. Rediscover parts you missed so you can gain the most from this work.

Visit www.Mein-Kampf-Audio.com for details

Dissecting The Hitler Mind-
Sex – Violent Childhood – Fear – Fits of Rage – Belief in Destiny They all played a part in creating the personality of Adolf Hitler. Psychoanalysis combined with hundreds of interviews with those close to Hitler have reverse-engineered the mind of Hitler in this professional psychological analysis. It reveals many previously unknown characteristics plus answers the question, "What was the *first more or less political activity..*" Hitler mentions in Mein Kampf. Includes pdf of the book and almost 7 hours of MP3 audio.

Find out more at www.HitlerLibrary.org

Official Nazi English Translation Of *Mein Kampf*
First time published outside of Nazi Germany! Rare version recently discovered. Originally liberated from a POW camp in Germany. This is the only English translation officially created by the Nazi Propaganda Ministry and printed on Nazi printing presses. Find out how to get your copy at

www.HitlerLibrary.org

MEIN KAMPF

Introduction

There are many secrets in the pages of *Mein Kampf*. In this critical analysis of the existing English translations, we will reveal errors that have distorted and obscured the meaning of the work. We will also explain some important points about *Mein Kampf* that have confused readers in the past and give you some background information that will enhance the political and historical meaning of *Mein Kampf*.

Take a quick look at the Appendix now. It documents and corrects many errors in past translations. Then return here to continue.

Many people have started reading *Mein Kampf*, but only a small percentage actually finished it. This is because the old translations were so hard to read. The sentences were complex and the text was filled with unfamiliar words, people, and places. The problem occurs when the reader tries to read more than one or two paragraphs. The reader is hit over the head with unusual and confusing words. Then the reader faces complex sentences with ten or more clauses. Some sentences are as long as a paragraph with one continuous thought, often with thirty or more words per sentence. After a few pages, the average reader became mentally exhausted and confused causing him or her to give up. The older English translations have resulted in *Mein Kampf* being inaccurately characterized as a ranting, disjointed work.

Fortunately this problem has been solved. The first new English translation in over 65 years has been released and it is the easiest to understand and the most accurate.

We will compare this new translation to older translations and the original German language version. But first, I want to share with you some secrets about *Mein Kampf* that most readers do not know.

This analysis is not designed to impose any opinions or make judgments about the content of Hitler's writings or the morality of the Nazi movement. This analysis does not promote racism or Nazism. This is a straightforward technical analysis of the work itself and is for educational purposes.

You know the old saying, if you do not learn from the past, it is bound to be repeated, and so it has proven true. We have seen the lessons in *Mein Kampf* repeat many times over as dictators have followed its teachings to gain power. By learning from *Mein Kampf* we can at least hope to identify dangerous dictators in the future, possibly before they are a threat. By ignoring the lessons in *Mein Kampf*, only dictators will gain from the information it contains and only they will have the advantage it offers to those seeking power.

Many people think *Mein Kampf* is a long diatribe against Jews and other races. The truth is that only a small part of *Mein Kampf* is anti-Semitic. The majority of it involves Hitler's discussion of the German people's difficult times after the First World War, his political

MEIN KAMPF

theories and his organization of the Nazi Party as well as many attacks against his enemies which makes it very interesting.

It is a mistake to answer the question "Why did the Nazis kill Jews?" with a simplistic answer of "the Nazi's were evil" or the even more foolish answer "they hated Jews", those are the kinds of answers a small child would propose and to over simplify the Holocaust with such trivial responses is to degrade its importance. In order to understand the true reason Hitler persecuted Jews and why thousands of his followers religiously pursued the extermination plan with vigor you must first understand what they believed and what they believed they were fighting for. They believed their actions were not just for themselves but for the world. Adolf Hitler revealed everything in *Mein Kampf* and the greater goals made perfect sense to the German people. They were willing to pursue those goals even if they did not agree with everything he said.

History can be boring to some, but do not let the fact that *Mein Kampf* contains a great deal of history and foreign policy fool you into thinking it is boring This book is NOT boring. This is not a text book. It is filled with a strong sense of heroism and a desire to support the underdog and, most of all, it is a fight for survival, at least in Hitler's view. Hitler was literally speaking to the common man in his words and he was motivating them, just as in his speeches. He makes foreign policy fascinating through his 'interpretation' and it is interesting to read or listen to Hitler's descriptions of what was really happening, at least from his point of view. To say the French sent troops into the Ruhr Area, is boring and dry, but when Hitler discusses what was done, the government incompetence he saw and how it affected the people, and then he calls for the people to rise up and heroically take the sword of vengeance in their hand, the entire event comes to life. You can see the factory smokestacks of the Ruhr as the French troops surround the buildings, you can see German Chancellor Cuno refusing to negotiate with the French, Hitler then explains why Cuno's plan of passive resistance was destined to fail, which it did. The frustration, then anger, it is all expressed with mastery by Hitler who was not speaking only for himself, but his thoughts were already shared by much of Germany. It is a moving story about the desire to return to the people of a country their self-respect and freedom.

Mein Kampf is an interesting phenomenon. No one would think anything about sitting in a public place and reading the *Communist Manifesto*, the *Turner Diaries*, or any of hundreds of other political or racially charged books, yet *Mein Kampf* is something people hide and read in private. They hesitate to tell their friends they have read it, but it has remained a bestseller. Quoting *Mein Kampf* in any school essay or term paper will garner suspicion from the instructor, possibly generate a visit to the principal, and even result in a lower grade than the one deserved. Any teacher who gave *Mein Kampf* as a reading assignment would be immediately fired while it is unlikely the administrator who made the firing decision would have even read the book. Quote *Mein Kampf* during an office meeting and it can cause the speaker to be labeled a racist by co-workers even if the quote has nothing to do with race at all. Of course, these condemnations are made by people who have not read *Mein Kampf.* '

You can stand on a street corner and quote Stalin, Lenin, Caesar, Martin Luther(an anti-

MEIN KAMPF

Semite who influenced Hitler), Jack the Ripper, Vlad Dracula without anyone even paying attention, but when you quote Hitler, the police will be called immediately. The reason has absolutely nothing to do with *Mein Kampf*. It has only to do with the reactions people have to what they think it contains. They do not want to be bothered with the facts, if they were, they might have to change their opinion and if they did that, they would have to admit they were previously wrong, so they prefer not to corrupt their beliefs with the facts of the matter. *Mein Kampf* is a personal and political work. It does contain some anti-Semitic passages, however they are a small part of the book. Hitler spends as much, possibly more, time attacking France than the Jews.

Hitler almost never uses truly racist remarks. He actually avoids using the German equivalent of the word 'racist'. The language on one of today's late night T.V. show can be more offensive, and the language of almost all stand up comedians is much more offensive. This fact is often overlooked by people who are unable to separate the book from the actions which took place almost 20 years after it was written. They tend to lump Hitler's life into one big ball and say, *well, he was evil later so nothing he said earlier can have any value.*

Mein Kampf is a large work that offers an interesting interpretation of politics, people, and foreign policy matters. To characterize it as simply a racist work is to oversimplify its message. Germany did not follow Hitler because he was a racist, they followed him because he promised a great future, and *Mein Kampf* is where he promised that great future.

It is important to understand that reading anti-Semitic passages or passages on race will not turn anyone into an anti-Semite. You do not have to worry about being filled with hatred simply by reading *Mein Kampf;* it is not a magic tome. Some people have so little faith in their own beliefs that they fear any exposure to *Mein Kampf* might twist them into something evil. If their beliefs are so fragile, so easily twisted, then they are already evil.

Unfortunately, many people are afraid that if they do not violently reject anything connected to *Mein Kampf*, and reject it in a showy way so that everyone sees their public display of rejection, then it somehow means they approve of the Holocaust. Of course, that is not logical reasoning and it seems silly when it is spelled out, but people often live by their gut reaction and do not think about *why* they dislike *Mein Kampf*—a book they never read— they just know they '*do*' or that they '*should*'. They are driven by fear, which leads to a hatred of *Mein Kampf* without a rational basis and without the need to read it in order to understand what it says. They want to live in a simple world where they can conveniently dismiss Hitler as a raving lunatic along with anyone else who does not immediately jump up at the mention of his name to join in the shouting match.

Anyone who is not already anti-Semitic, will usually find the racist passages somewhere between comical and offensive. In the areas where non-Aryan races are discussed, it is like watching a really bad play which goes on and on trying to explain itself while nothing of consequence actually happens. Many Nazi followers before World War II had the same experience when confronted with the Nazi political platform. They did not follow or believe in the party because of its racist views, they were themselves not all anti-Semitic, but they supported the Nazi party because of everything else it represented, nationalism, social improvement, freedom (from other countries), strength, regaining the nation's self-respect. They chose to ignore the racist parts of the party platform and focused on the political and social aspects. Someone who is already a racist will only find confirmation of their existing beliefs. To someone who is not racist, they will mostly be bemused at Hitler's comments about Jews and other non-Aryan races.

It would be foolish to dismiss Hitler as 'just a madman'. Ask yourself, how many madmen rise from living in a flop house to ruling a country as supreme, unquestioned dictator. There is more to be learned here and anyone who ignores these lessons, does so at their own peril and the peril of all civilization. It is important to understand the lessons of *Mein Kampf* because only through understanding can the signs of the next threat be recognized.

Mein Kampf is an odd mix of brilliant ideas and bizarre ideas. These are so different it is hard to come to terms with the fact they came from the same person. One moment Hitler describes a fanciful childlike dream about how a nation's economy should be structured in the feudal way of the past, something that anyone could see would not work, and in the next section he explains how to structure a fanatical movement that will survive and grow with frightening insight into human nature and with revelations that are so obvious, you will wonder why you did not see those truths before.

Hitler's expansive ideas of a massive Jewish plan become more fanciful as the 'plot' grows to include every inch of the world, their plan to topple the Japanese, to rule Europe, but this all played into the overall image of his effort to save the world. Whether Hitler believed it was true or not was unimportant. The Jewish antagonist was necessary for his propaganda effort. He needed an enemy to fight, and as he said himself, "*...a nation must see one single enemy, not multiple enemies, otherwise they will question the justness of their own cause.*"

Due to his disagreements with Karl Harrer (a founding member of the DAP party who thought Hitler's propaganda was crossing into deception), it appears Hitler may himself have not believed some of his grandiose theories about Jewish plans for world domination, but they were necessary to form a solid front. Hitler needed one enemy to fight and the Jews were the perfect choice because he could point to any nation, any action and say the Jews were behind it. This gave him one consolidated enemy, which is also clearly spelled out in his own propaganda.

However we must not become sidetracked, as so many are, with the racist parts of *Mein Kampf*. We must not forget that this is the how-to manual from a man who went from being a destitute artist to ruling a nation, not by chance, but by following his thought out plan, a plan he has revealed in *Mein Kampf*.

It is important to remember that when *Mein Kampf* was written, Hitler was not the undisputed leader of anything. His party had been disbanded and outlawed. He was in danger of losing his position. *Mein Kampf* was meant as a political tool to be used within his own group to help him maintain power. It was intended to show himself as the great leader, to distance himself from the bourgeois parties, and to make it clear he was a fanatic radical. If he had been anything less, his followers would have abandoned him.

The two most common ways of dealing with *Mein Kampf* have been to make it freely available or to lock it away from everyone. Making *Mein Kampf* freely available allows people to see it for what it is. Those who want to lock it away believe absolute suppression will somehow prevent anyone from following the same plan again. Suppression is pointless. With the ability to beam information around the world in seconds, there is no such thing. To make it available and explain it is a much better option and that is what we are doing here.

When reading *Mein Kampf*, you will find yourself saying frequently "that is certainly true" because much of what he says is true, at least from a certain point of view. Some is an oversimplification of history or politics as well and it is all engineered to show his side favorably and the opponent unfavorably, which is the purpose of his work of propaganda.

Mein Kampf taps into fundamental human concepts of heroism, survival, fear, being the underdog, the promise of a great future. These are all themes that have a strong appeal to human nature and explain in part the appeal Hitler had in his speeches. What makes *Mein Kampf* more powerful is the knowledge that it is real. It is not a novel about a fantasy world or the theories of a political philosopher, it is about events and feelings that existed in Germany, things an entire nation lived through and suffered under, and many of those same feelings and beliefs exist in countries around the world today.

Understanding *Mein Kampf*

There are people who have criticized Hitler for the quality of his writing. Hitler did not write *Mein Kampf*, he dictated it. Hitler was a speaker, not a writer. Choices for punctuation and even wording were altered or added by the person taking down what Hitler dictated, not Hitler. The book does not even appear to have been edited heavily before being published. It is also believed that his secretary, Hess, may have filled in parts he did not have time to type based on his knowledge of Hitler's speeches.

Mein Kampf has the feel of a first draft. It is unlikely it was edited any more than minor grammatical fixes. How it came out of Hitler's mouth is how it went on the page and no one dared to change more than a spelling correction without Hitler's prior approval once it was on paper. As far as first-drafts go, it is a good first draft.

Mein Kampf must be looked at as if it were a long speech. Some have criticized Hitler for the way he orders his words, however this criticism comes mainly from English speakers who have read the older English translations or those who are not native German speakers and learned German language from books. In German, as in English, it is not uncommon to *order words oddly*.

The choice of word order is a matter of style and a poet often uses unusual word arrangements. This was Hitler's method and it was how he kept his audience's attention. You must also remember that Hitler was speaking to the masses, those in the public working classes, who were less educated. These were the people in his organization. They came from these masses. So, just as Hitler said, he targeted his words specifically to this group. He picked his style to match his audience.

It is quite inappropriate to criticize Hitler's style today. For one, his writing was in German and if a person is not a native, lifelong German speaker, he could not fully appreciate the language itself or its nuances. Even in English, if we look back at books written in English in the 1920's, the English language appears most unusual. They use different phrases which were common at the time, different references, different assumptions about how the audience would interpret their writing, and words that are practically unknown today.

Language changes quickly and what was perfectly acceptable in 1920 in English is considered poor or even ignorant style today. Anyone who is not German and did not live in the 1920's cannot criticize the language style of a German book written in the 1920's when English books themselves have many unusual characteristics from the same period. Some believe if they can criticize the style and grammar, that somehow affects the ideas. Actually, that is not even true. These critics do not care about the actual ideas in *Mein Kampf*, they only want to criticize the "group idea" which is the idea that everyone has about *Mein Kampf*, which has nothing to do with the book's actual contents. They dislike the author and what he did and because of that, many people feel they should dislike his book, and they are afraid that if they do not dislike his book, that somehow others will see that as approval of his message.

MEIN KAMPF

Some German sayings have been lost in older translations and some translators, like James Murphy, made up their own sayings to replace German sayings. Those replacements did not always match the original meaning. Some of the older translations also made "corrections" to Hitler's work which altered the meaning.

The word Jew or any variation of it (Jewish or Jewry etc.) is used 547 times. This is only 4.4% of the book (*based on an average of 20 words per sentence and assuming the word Jew or variations appears an average of once per sentence*). The word negro (*which was not necessarily offensive at the time*) appears 20 times which is 0.16% of the book. The word nigger is never used and neither are any common vulgarities other than a "damned well better" usage which occurs once. Hitler does use the term Hottentot twice which could be considered offensive, though it was common at the time just as we would say "Indian" to mean Native American today. The same is true for several other ethnic groups which were named but not necessarily with an offensive name. Hitler rarely used offensive words in his speeches and used the word *Jüdlein* (*equivalent to Kike*) only once in *Mein Kampf*, otherwise using *Juden (Jew)* or variations of it.

The majority of the book is about Hitler, his political beliefs, the German nation and the building of the Nazi party. Make no mistake though, there are passages where Hitler does criticize the Jews and blames them for economic problems, accuses them of controlling the press and attempting to destroy the world. I am not trying to say this is not part of the book or to minimize it, just to say there is more in Neapolitan ice-cream than vanilla.

Mein Kampf has approximately 245,244 words total (this number is from the Ford Translation which will be used in all statistics).

Word Occurrence Counts:
- The word Jew or Jewish or Jewry is used 547 times
- negro appears 20 times
- nigger does not appear at all
- Marxist appears 135 times
- populist(meaning racialist) appears 98 times
- race appears 339 times
- political appears 447 times
- France appears 129 times
- war appears 450 times
- hero appears 103 times

Today, with the availability of the History Channel and countless Internet resources, the average person is much more informed and much more aware of history which makes the holes in many of Hitler's Jewish theories quite obvious. Again, I am not trying to minimize his anti-Semitism. I am trying to point out the world Hitler spoke to in 1924 and the world of today are quite different. The Jews played an important role in his rhetoric. His story needed a villain to rally against and that is how he used them. They became the unseen Black Hand behind every ill event and at that time in Germany the people were ready to accept that theory. Hitler was not the first to propose his racial theories. They existed in various movements, but he was the first to consolidate them into a modernized version that appealed to large numbers of people, along with other elements of the movement.

We often see in documentaries quotes about the "Jewish Question". This actually results from a translation between German and English. To say question instead of problem makes it sound like a euphemism to say the Jewish "question", but it is actually nothing more than a translation anomaly where the German word for question and problem are the same and the choice depends on the context when it is translated into English. Hitler also made reference to the "prostitution question" and other problem/questions. There is no direct German translation for the English word *Problem,* but question translates to *Frage* which is not the word used. Many translators simply translate this into Jewish Question when the true meaning is Jewish Problem. Hitler and the Nazi's were not trying to be obtuse or to obscure their meaning by using Jewish Question, they said what they meant, Jewish Problem, but it was poorly translated into English. In English we can say "solve this math problem" but it would be equally accurate to say "answer this math question". It is the same in German and the translation choice into English determines how problem or question is used.

Frage is question in German, and it is also used for Problem English. *Aufgabe* is problem in German but it usually means task when it is used. It would have been just as accurately translated as *Jewish Problem*. The meaning is the same but you should be aware that problem and question have the same meaning here. The term "Jewish Question" has become so synonymous with the Nazi party that it has continued to be used.

If you do not know what Aryan means, then some parts of *Mein Kampf* may be confusing. Hitler believed that in the past there was one great founding race of people on earth called the Aryans which 'seeded' all other cultures because the Aryan culture was the only one capable of creating culture. Without this mythical Aryan influence, other cultures would simply decline and die. No such race actually existed. When Hitler speaks of the great race that spawns cultures, he means the mythical Aryan race.

Mein Kampf contains many contradictions:

- In one place he says Jews control the Marxist press which attacks the bourgeois press, but then later he says the Jews also control the bourgeois press.

- Hitler says Marxist doctrine is hidden under a cover various times, but then it is in full public view. Here is a section where he says both at the same time: '*Under this covering of purely social ideas we find that extremely evil intentions are present. In fact, they are openly presented, in full public view, with the most bold insolence.*'

- Hitler complains about single parliamentarians trying to convince the crowd of parliament that their point of view is valid and their ability to do their job depended on their ability to convince others more ignorant than themselves their point of view was right, but his own system of government which was to replace the existing parliament involves a crowd of advisors who each try to convince the chairman of the committee that their idea is valid so he can make a decision instead of a decision being made by a vote of the crowd, which is basically the same evil he was preaching against only reversed.

- Hitler says he did not discuss political matters during war but then later he says [on the front] 'I openly expressed my beliefs to my close army friends quite often.'

There are many contradictions which can be found like these.

Hitler's economic and educational plans are crude especially in comparison to his understanding of the requirements of an extremist political movement. He understands how to build a fanatical political organization and the use of propaganda very well but lacks a basic understanding of economics or the education system when explaining his theories of how the new National Socialist government would implement his policies. His basic plans were to return Germany to a feudal society of peasant farmers and to end education for the masses except for basic vocational training while replacing education time with exercise time.

Hitler talks at length about the cultural and intellectual development of the race and how important it is, yet, when he came to power, his own education program completely halted all cultural and intellectual training including ending intellectual classes, requiring classes to be rewritten to focus on Nazi goals, and an end to philosophy and psychology studies if they were not of immediate benefit to the Nazi party. Here is a quote from *Mein Kampf*; "It does not merely assure the preservation of this nationality, but the state must lead the people to the highest freedom possible by continuing to develop its spiritual and intellectual capacities." This goal was changed to an extreme degree and all education was replaced by the teaching of Nazi values.

Some criticize Hitler for using mixed metaphors. This is rather petty in itself because mixed metaphors were not uncommon in the German press at the time and are common even today. It is the equivalent of saying, 'My God, did he end a sentence with a preposition?' which is hardly a condemnable act even if it may not be considered perfect grammar. Hitler's words were for the less educated classes of his followers and it would have been inappropriate for his words to be perfect. To criticize his work in this way is the equivalent of saying, 'I wouldn't do it that way so it must be wrong.' Some have pointed out that Hitler's prose lacks the eloquence of Lenin, but Lenin wrote for the intellectuals, not the common man. The difference is between a thinker and a doer. Such criticisms are attempts to discredit his work without resorting to understanding it first.

> Here is an example of one of his mixed metaphors where he starts with mushrooms and ends with squeak: *'Such societies sprang up like mushrooms everywhere, but disappeared without a squeak after a short time.'*

Hitler often based his theories on pseudo-scientific ideas. I say pseudo-scientific because he took leading edge scientific ideas which were then modified by others into concepts often very far from their original intent. For instance Hitler promoted an idea of Geographical Politics which is presumably a scientific attempt to show that a nation's strength and longevity is determined by the area it occupies. He also used Darwin's theory of evolution but only after it had been re-interpreted by other fringe scientists. Many of Hitler's theories about Jews also came from American anti-Semitic papers. His flawed economic theories, which he later abandoned, came from Gottfried Feder and claimed any charging of interest in the loaning of money was usury and should be illegal. This is actually an old religious idea in Europe. He also believed in making small cities that were self sufficient, as I previously said, it was a return to feudal society. Hitler promotes Feder and his theories in *Mein Kampf* but later was forced to abandon the ideas as unworkable.

Some words can have multiple meanings. For instance, in German spiritual often means moral. The word peoples or people can be interchanged with nations, states, or even race. Often when Hitler talks about peoples or people he means the dominant race, not just the country. The interpretation depends on the surrounding argument.

In America, we generally consider 'state' as a reference to a subdivision of the nation, however in Europe, state is commonly used to describe a country. Hitler frequently uses state to refer to the German National State. What Americans might consider individual states are provinces in Europe(a subdivision of a nation or state), but these can also be called states, the government within a country and other countries themselves can also be states. So don't be confused when you see the word state, it usually means country or national government but can mean smaller subdivisions of the nation.

There are other phrases Hitler uses which should be explained such as *cosmopolitan Jew* which means a Jew of many aspects, due to their worldwide nature and their integration and knowledge of cultures and ability to speak languages worldwide (there was no Jewish state at the time *Mein Kampf* was written). The Reynal-Hitchcock translation sometimes simplified the term into the shorter 'world Jew' or 'international Jew' however international cosmopolitan Jew has a larger meaning so the true meaning is lost if it is trimmed down to a simple word without the reader understanding what word is being replaced and what it really means.

One very important thing to keep in mind when reading *Mein Kampf* is that events did not always unfold in the simplistic way Hitler describes and did not happen as he states. They were often more complicated and had many people on both sides. For instance, he repeatedly attacks the bourgeois for their cowardice and inability to make decisions. This however was only the image he wanted the reader to have. In fact, some bourgeois societies were highly nationalistic and violent, consisting of ex-soldiers, certainly not cowards, and some of his rival political movements were very militant, some more militant than the Nazi party.

Hitler's interpretation of history was also meant to serve his purpose. He is writing a book which is itself propaganda and not a history book. He attacks Chancellor Cuno's plan for passive resistance after the French invasion of the Ruhr area. There is no evidence Hitler spoke against this action at the time, however in *Mein Kampf* he says he warned everyone

MEIN KAMPF

of what would happen and that his predictions came true exactly as he said. Many of his foreign policy theories also are over simplifications about events of the time. For example, his claims that the military was weak and no one in charge knew what they were doing, however this is unfounded because the pre-war leaders had put a lot of effort into the military and had their own ideas about world conquest. When reading *Mein Kampf*, keep in mind that the historical references may not be fully accurate, though they are still very instructive and you will learn a lot about foreign policy, how to think about foreign policy, and the consequences of bad foreign policy.

The original party which Hitler joined was called the DAP or Deutsche Arbeiter Partei. Later, in 1920, he renamed the party as the NSDAP or National Socialist German Workers' Party in English or in German it is Nationalsozialistische Deutsche Arbeiterpartei (NSDAP). In English this is shortened to Nazi Party. It is sometimes abbreviated using the English letters as NSGWP.

The D.A.P. or German Worker's Party Hitler originally joined offers some additional examples of inconsistencies. Hitler makes the party sound like they were sitting around doing nothing until he showed up and took charge. This is a revision of history. What annoyed Drexler was Hitler's down-playing of Drexler's role because he was the real founder of the D.A.P. not Hitler. *Mein Kampf* is not a historical book. It is as much propaganda as anything else.

Hitler claimed he was the seventh member of the DAP. This is another area where there are inconsistencies in *Mein Kampf*. He was actually the seventh member of the committee, not the party. In volume two of *Mein Kampf* he says that he joined the six man party in autumn of 1919, however his membership card (which was apparently later forged to say seven instead of 555 - numbering started at 500) showed otherwise and a letter from Drexler later complained about his claim that he was the seventh member and said he was actually member fifty-five, not seven. There is some question about the accuracy of this because membership cards were not issued in order of joining; they were issued in alphabetical order. Hitler may have interpreted his joining as the seventh *active* member and ignored the others who were showing up at meetings. Also Hitler first says the party had nothing printed not even membership cards, yet he later says after he joined he received his card immediately. This statement is also unclear. Since cards were issued in alphabetical order, it is possible they were not issued until later and then issued by going through the files and distributed to everyone at once. Hitler said the party had no membership cards when they are first mentioned, but then at the end of chapter nine of volume one he says "I applied for membership in the German Workers' Party and received a provisional membership certificate bearing the number seven!" The decision to join was made two days after he attended the first meeting so they would have had to have obtained membership cards for everyone in that short time but again later he says the did not have them until after he joined. It is confusing.

MEIN KAMPF

Here is part of Drexler's letter:

> *No one knows better than you yourself, my Führer, that you were never the seventh member of the party, but at best the seventh member of the committee, which I asked you to join as recruitment director. And a few years ago I had to complain to a party office that your first proper membership card of the DAP, bearing the signatures of Schüssler and myself, was falsified, with the number 555 being erased and number 7 entered. (Kershaw, Hitler: Hubris 1889-1936, Penguin Books, p. 127).*

Further, Hitler says at the first meeting he attended, he was handed a printed red book. Then a few paragraphs later when describing his attendance of the second meeting he again says they had noting printed at all, yet he already said he was handed a booklet about the party.

In volume one, Hitler says that he first went to Sterneckerbräu Beer Hall for the very first meeting of the DAP before he joined and a second time for the Feder lecture. Then later in volume two he says the party only met previously in a cafe and the Herrengasse meeting room and that he went out and found the Sterneckerbräu for their use as an office.

Many of Hitler's *recollections* are modified to improve his image. For example he claims that at the first party meeting he attended, he asked some highly targeted and intelligent questions to the amazement of those in attendance and then Anton Drexler ran up to him and shoved a booklet in his hand as he was leaving. But, another account says '*Adolf Hitler sprang up from the audience to rebut the argument. Drexler approached Hitler and thrust a booklet into his hand.*' Both describe the same situation but the second account, which was told by a different person, could easily be interpreted as meaning Drexler was upset with Hitler's ignorance and his thrusting of the book was meant to say '*learn something before opening your mouth next time.*' Hitler's retelling of events at meetings and other instances are often adjusted for his benefit or for purposes of propaganda.

Mein Kampf is often criticized because of historical inaccuracies yet when compared to any history text book, you can identify one-for-one an inaccuracy in the textbook and find the average history book is equally inaccurate or self serving based on the country where it was published. In France, many of Napoleon's greatest defeats are taught as his greatest victories while the same battles are described as great defeats in American history books. Two history books with two opposite conclusions and many times neither is fully right or wrong. It is inaccurate to dismiss Hitler's view of history as wrong simply because it disagrees with some history books. Anyone who lived through some particular event and then reads about it in the newspaper or history books can immediately see inaccuracies and obvious omissions that other readers are unaware of. The same can be said of Hitler's writing when compared to historical references which we today only refer to. So, Hitler's references may not be considered historically accurate, however that does not necessarily make it wrong.

Hitler paints all other political parties with a broad brush. They are all wrong, incompetent, old men wearing monocles and cowardly intellectuals who cannot do the job. Only his party has a chance of success, according to Hitler. He uses the same broad labeling method to discuss historical events.

It was Hitler's intention to portray himself and his movement as heroic. He took liberties with facts and circumstances to create this image. This is exactly what we would expect because the work is itself propaganda.

It is important to remember that Hitler's interpretation and retelling of history or events is often intentionally distorted to prove the point he wishes to make. This explains why there are some inconsistencies. He may want to prove one point early in the book and a slightly different point later which means he must adjust the facts a little. He may ignore some facts or give an interpretation as the only one when counter interpretations fit the facts better.

In the second volume is where you truly begin to hear his strong appeal. His speaking style improved between 1924 and 1926 when the second volume was published. His grandiose statements, if you imagine them being played to a large audience, are clearly emotionally appealing and the image he paints of a great future for everyone and a future that is only opposed by the chance of total destruction would draw anyone into the world he creates. There is a noticeable difference between volume one (written 1924) and volume two (published 1926). You can see a more refined and developed style which, even in written form, inspires the audience. Volume two is the real Hitler who influenced a nation with his powerful speeches.

When Hitler says International he means Marxists or those who follow the international Jew, international financiers, as well as those outside the country who control and manipulate national matters. A nationalist is a patriot who keeps control of country assets within the country and wants a strong military, which is a very Prussian attitude so they were often associated with Prussians.

There are some interesting errors in *Mein Kampf*. Several sentences in the original German were so complex they were unclear even to Germans so they were omitted or reworded in later editions. Some names were removed as well such as Henry Ford, the car maker. This may have been at his request, but it is more likely Hitler had his name removed after Henry Ford made a public apology to the Jews over his anti-Semitic newspaper. The first volume listed sixteen men in the dedication, yet in the first print run of volume two Hitler says he wants to refer back to those eighteen men. He was likely thinking of two additional party members who died later. This error was fixed by the second printing. Some names were dropped in later editions because they were simply unimportant in Hitler's opinion such as newspaper magnate Northcliffe's name.

Marxists are also called Reds, internationals, republicans. All of these also refer to Jews. Republic refers to the new Marxist parliamentary republic established in Germany as a result of the 1918 Marxist revolution which occurred with the end of the First World War.

November criminals refers to the idea that those who participated in the November 1918 revolution were crooks who betray the country. Hitler repeatedly refers to this event.

MEIN KAMPF

The original German text uses *bourgeois* or in German it is *Bürgertum*, and middle class or petite-bourgeois in German is *Spießbürgers*. The Manheim translation used shopkeeper for middle class sometimes (Spießbürgers). The word bourgeois can have various meanings depending on who is using it. Any instances of bourgeois in *Mein Kampf* may be more accurately called leader-class or wealthy-aristocrat but this is not completely accurate. Generally it means someone of privilege who is in an upper social class and has acquired wealth undeservedly. Government officials and nobles, sometimes white collar workers like school administrators or other high level jobs can also be included. In the Ford translation, bourgeois was changed to privileged-class and petty bourgeois to middle-class. In this context, "aristocrats" does not mean by royal birth, but those who inherited or otherwise have money. Hitler talks very little about the real middle-class and mostly about the proletariat masses or the bourgeois upper/ruling classes. Some people assume bourgeois means middle class but this is inaccurate at least in the context of *Mein Kampf*. It would be more accurate to think of a very large proletariat class, a very small middle class and a slightly smaller bourgeois class which was more visible. The middle class was not as dominant as it is today. In Marxism, bourgeois means someone who is part of a property owning class so you can consider middle and leader-class to mean property owners or an exploiter of the worker. Hitler adapted his meaning from the Marxist meaning. Bourgeoisie (ending in –geoisie) is a member of that class also could be business class. Bourgeois is uncommon in English speaking countries but more common in other countries.

Hitler discussed syphilis at length. There is much controversy over why he spent so many pages on the matter. Medical reports discovered after World War II indicated that he may have suffered from syphilis. At any rate, he believed he had syphilis and his doctor administered treatments that were common for syphilis suffers at the time. This could explain why he was so concerned with the disease and felt it was important enough to devote an extensive section of *Mein Kampf* to.

Hitler uses the word propaganda frequently. In English the word propaganda carries negative connotations, however the way Hitler uses it, he means an idea along the lines of education, political-advertising, promoting your ideology or more specifically indoctrination.

Hitler disliked interest, meaning the charging of a fee to loan money (including buying corporate stock, bonds and other financial instruments). This was a matter that was of great concern during the Protestant reformation in Europe, which is something that influenced Hitler. Previously, the Catholic Church banned the charging of interest as usury or theft. Of course, the result was economic stagnation. Calin's reformations changed this by declaring interest as part of work and work was Godly which opened up many new business opportunities and greatly enhanced commerce because money was no longer sitting idly in bank vaults. Hitler's idea dates back to the previous misguided concept of a *simpler time*.

Hitler talks about International Finance money and financial sectors. What this really means is the type of money that is generated from interest and interest generating financial sectors, stocks, bonds, as opposed to hourly labor wages. The theories these ideas are based on are a misguided understanding of financial systems which only works if you have a government controlled agricultural and factory based economy which effectively keeps everyone poor. In the 1920's, many aspects of economics were still mysteries. Eliminating interest money effectively ends the possibility of improvement and only allows an economy to grow through a wartime boom. Early on, this was Hitler's goal, a feudal type of society based on agriculture.

It is often claimed that Hitler was an Atheist. After reading *Mein Kampf* it is clear he believed in a God and Heaven, and especially in a fate or more accurately a plan for our destiny that involves self determinism. Claims that he was an Atheist are frequently used to distance him from any religion. No one wants to say they have the same religion as Hitler.

Hitler was a non-practicing Catholic and even considered becoming a member of the clergy in his later youth when he attended a religious school. The claim of Atheism is made on its own, with no support. None is needed with such a broad claim and any attempt to validate the claim is easily disproved. It automatically, in theory, accounts for all of his actions therefore it is reasoned there is no need to dig deeper into the man. People spend time researching his history, where he was, what he said, but they ignore his own book and the words he uses in it. The nail in the coffin of the Atheist argument is when in 1933 Hitler said in a speech. '*I am now and have always been a Catholic and I plan to remain one.*' He may not have been active in the church, but that does not make him an Atheist.

Hitler's ideas were a collection of ideas he picked up from other writers and theoreticians. His ideas on anti-Semitism, Pan-German movements, expansion, etc. were not his original ideas but were widely distributed by race-conscious newspapers of pre-First World War Germany. Hitler did however give them a strong voice, consolidated them into one idea facing a single enemy, and turned them into coherent propaganda that could be used to motivate the masses.

His gift was the ability to piece them together and to motivate the people to, if not follow, at least not obstruct his movement. Some have tried to criticize Hitler for his adoption of the ideas by other people, however the same can be said for any philosopher or any politician. It would be abnormal for a man who was an artist to wake up one day and know the great course for a country with all of the details worked out, all without ever researching the political ideas/opinions of others. Some try to say Hitler had no original ideas when the truth is very few people have had any original ideas. They are based on the writings and thoughts of other people who pieced them together from yet others. Hitler took a set of long existing ideas, turned them into a form with which modern people would identify, created a political platform that people would follow, and motivated them to put those ideas into practice. It does not matter that he was inspired by others, what he did with ideas which had been passed around for hundreds of years with little result is what separates his writing and speeches from the work of others.

A number of top Nazi leaders were known to have never read *Mein Kampf*. This is sometimes used to criticize the book. However, they listened to hundreds of Hitler's speeches which had the same basic content. They did not need to read the book because they had heard it many times over.

Known Translations

There have been various English translations of *Mein Kampf* and some foreign translations were based on the English versions. These have been dogged by criticism since they were released. I will not go into excessive details on these translations but will give a quick summary of each. I will also not discuss the foreign language translations because they vary so much. However, many foreign language(other than English) translations were based on poor English translations and not the original German. They were created by people who spoke English as a second language and had great difficulty understanding the unusual words and complex sentences of older English translations. As a result, many foreign language versions are filled with errors and excessive embellishments.

You can find more information on the various editions in the

Mein Kampf: **A Collectors Guide eBook from www.HitlerLibrary.org**

Dugdale Translation 1933

The first legal translation was an abridged(incomplete) edition called the Dugdale translation. It was criticized for selectively omitting sections, however the omissions appear to be random. The quality of the translation was not up to par, that combined with public complaints about an abridged version led to a new translation. The Dugdale version was published by Hurst & Blackett in London and Houghton Mifflin in the US.

Here is a Dugdale example compared to the **Ford translation:**

> **Dugdale-Translation:** I refused to countenance such folly, and after a very short time I ceased to attend the meetings of the committee. I made my propaganda for myself, and that was an end of it; I refused to allow any ignoramus to talk me into any other course.

> **Ford translation:** I refused to submit to such foolishness and after a very short time, I stopped attending the committee sessions. I prepared my propaganda and that was that. I also did not let some good-for-nothing interfere with my work, just as I did not concern myself with their business.

The Dugdale quote appears to say that Hitler was producing propaganda for himself. Although we can figure out it means, this is not what was originally intended or written. The Dugdale translation not only omitted paragraphs, it omitted important sentences and critical information from within sentences in an effort to abridge the book as much as possible. Dugdale was significant because it was the first legally published copy of *Mein*

MEIN KAMPF

Kampf, but it is not commonly read today since unabridged(full) versions are available now. Considering the over-edited nature. Because it is abridged, it will not be used for any further examples or analysis in this text.

Official Nazi Murphy Translation 1936-37

James Murphy created a translation for the Nazi government. He had some sympathies for their politics and because of this the Nazi propaganda ministry hired him to create the English translation of *Mein Kampf*. He worked on this edition in Germany. Over time, Murphy's opinions about the Nazi government changed. The German government decided they no longer cared for him after he made some critical remarks and told him he had to leave. He left quickly without his translation into English. Later he sent his wife back and she was able to obtain a copy from his German secretary. The German government edited and published the Murphy version which was completed for them, in English, and it was printed within Germany from the presses of the Nazi printing office. Very few copies are known to have been printed. Some copies were sent to POW camps in Germany for British and American POW's. A very rare version of this official Nazi English edition has recently been re-discovered republished for the first time since it was printed by the Nazi government. It is very interesting to compare this translation to both Murphy's later British translation and to the new Ford translation to see the differences.

This edition had the regular British spellings(James Murphy was British) which were common for the time, *to-day* instead of today, and *labour* instead of labor. However, it also had many gross misspellings, punctuation errors, and grammar errors. Apparently an English speaking Nazi Party member took James Murphy's unpolished translation and tried to finish it.

Here are some examples of the errors in the Official Nazi Murphy Edition:

> For instance, intelligentsia is spelled as intelligentzia in the Nazi edition.
> "..the blackmailers that were arrested and *gaoled*." instead of *jailed* where gaoled is an archaic British term.
> "... I was *answerd* with a triple 'Heil'" notice misspelling.
> "...that we should `look out for *ouselves*' and..."
> The word *disintegration* is sometimes spelled correctly and sometimes spelled as *disintregation*.
> "..would turn out detrimental rather than helpful to the interests of that province- but through fear of an agreement *ment* being established between Germany.." this may be an editing error duplicating the end of agreement or a misspelling of meant.
> "I *endeavoured* to *instil* them gradually into the members of the young organization,..."
> "...can continue to play an important *rôle* in the world only if Germany be dismembered." Notice the unnecessary pronunciation mark in the word "role".

23

MEIN KAMPF

It would be a mistake to think this is a more accurate translation simply because it is the official Nazi version. The language differences and the poor translation plus the errors are quite jarring to the reader. It is best used as a reference or a comparison against other translations. It is entertaining to see how the Nazi party tried to explain *Mein Kampf* using English words familiar to themselves. Reading the official Nazi version after reading a good translation is quite interesting so I do recommend you pick up a copy and compare it to other translations. You will discover more about the text for yourself.

Murphy British Translation 1939

After Murphy was kicked out of Germany and he obtained a copy of his manuscript, he continued to work on it. He finalized a deal with Hurst & Blackett, but they ceased publishing the Murphy translation in 1942 when the original plates were destroyed by German bombing.

Murphy often embellished sections, adding references, and making it into his own style, not so much in Hitler's style. Murphy often used long, uncommon words which make the text hard to understand. Some of his words included fructified, fetters, propitious, milliards, recalcitrant, ineluctable, loquacious, and other words the average person would simply not recognize.

Murphy took artistic license in some of these descriptions and even with his German language skill, he did not fully understand the meaning of many passages he translated.

He captured the general ideas, but the nuance was lost. He added to descriptions to embellish them, but in doing so, he strayed from Hitler's style and sometimes from the meaning. Hitler often was very straight forward, using simple terms while Murphy used complex words. While Hitler aimed his message at the uneducated masses, Murphy wrote for the intellectual.

Murphy's word choices were often taken out of a German-English dictionary which meant he took the most common meaning, not necessarily the best meaning. For example, in one place Murphy uses the word 'devotion' when the true translation is closer to 'fanaticism' which alters the meaning significantly.

Reynal and Hitchcock Translation 1938

Houghton and Mifflin licensed Reynal & Hitchcock the rights to publish their version of the full unexpurgated translation in 1938. It was translated by a committee of men from the New School for Social Research and appeared on February 28, 1939. This description is misleading because some of the men on the *committee* had nothing to do with the actual translation. Some of the translation is believed to have been completed by assistants.

The Reynal translation was more of a line-for-line translation. It is true to the original to a fault. It is translated directly, sometimes in a way that makes the meaning unclear. The original German sentence structures were often preserved which makes it very difficult to read in English. Reynal also used many uncommon words. When the translators did not understand a passage, they simply translated it literally word-for-word using word substitution.

Stackpole Translation

Stackpole and Sons commissioned their own translation, without securing copyrights. This was before World War II started so Hitler still had a copyright claim. The entire copyright story is rather involved but interesting. The short version is that Reynal and Hitchcock contracted the rights for the authorized version from Hurst and Blackett so they had a legal claim in the US and stopped the publication of Stackpole's edition after 12,000 copies were printed. The Stackpole translation was rushed, it was inaccurate, and many sentences make no sense at all because they were translated without paying attention to the meaning. It looks like two different people translated it because there is a clear difference in the writing styles between first half of the book and the second half based on the pages, not Volume 1 and Volume 2. Very little is known about the technical work of the translation done by Stackpole. It is just as well that this version was not kept in print because it is one of the worst translations and is filled with errors. The book is considered collectible however.

Here is an example from the **Stackpole translation:**

> **Stackpole translation:** The world is ruled by only a fraction of all Wisdom, of which fraction almost any Ministerial Councillor embodies but one atom. Since Germany has become a Republic, however, this is no longer true-that is why the Law to Protect the Republic forbids any one to say or even to believe such a thing.

It says "this is no longer true", but the original German text and the clear meaning of the paragraph shows that it IS true. Such mistakes corrupt the meaning of the original writing and collectively make it confusing and unreadable. The Stackpole translation is filled with errors, sometimes many per page.

Here is another example from the Stackpole translation. This could have just as easily come from the Reynal or Manheim too.

> **Stackpole translation:** The further result is, however, that in so doing the danger of a battle of the defenders of the old State against those of the new seems once and for all to be diverted. One cannot emphasize this fact too often.

The use of the word *of* repeatedly creates a confusing sentence. Such choices make the translation hard to understand.

MEIN KAMPF

Manheim Translation

Houghton Mifflin commissioned a new translation by Ralph Manheim which was published in 1943. They created this new edition to avoid having to share their profits with Reynal & Hitchcock. They also wanted to offer a more readable translation. It was a definite improvement over past translations, however it still has many errors and fails to identify many critical references. It also mistranslates common sayings used by Hitler. Manheim used footnotes to indicate original German words in an effort to clarify the translation, however to a non German speaker this is not helpful and a German speaker would likely read the original German so these notes were not useful. Many items that should have been footnoted, such as people and places or sayings that were not familiar to English speakers, were not footnoted by Manheim. When Manheim was unsure of a word (for example Sheepshead meaning the Bavarian card game), he left it untranslated and inserted the original German words in the text. His translation contains many German words and sentences. Some passages are also missing from the Manheim translation, most likely because did not understand them. I conclude this because the missing passages are frequently complex statements that make more sense when spoken with inflection than when written.

Manheim's mechanical translation style also makes his translation difficult to read. Sentences are translated almost word for word from German without thought to word order or overall sentence meaning. The result is a jumbled and disjointed translation which is nothing like the original book.

The Manheim translation contains numerous typographical errors as well. For example, one line refers to a battle in "1948" which is long after Mein Kampf was written and obviously should have been 1848. In another place it says: "It would be a stake to think that the followers..." which should clearly have been "mistake", not "stake".

Ford Translation

This is the newest translation made in 2009. The past translations were mostly rushed to press with little time for editing and correction. The Ford translation was not rushed to press and was thoroughly researched. It is the first translation verified by actual German native speakers. This is the easiest to read translation ever made. It has revealed many elements of *Mein Kampf* which were not part of past translations including sayings by Hitler and his poetic style which were edited out of older translations. The Ford translation also maintains a high standard of accuracy. If Hitler used a particular word, then that word was used and not embellished into another word. Every definition was evaluated to make sure the correct translation was chosen, not just the common usage of a word. This translation is also the only *Mein Kampf* ever available as a full length audio book from www.Mein-Kampf-Audio.com

Translating any work is a major project. Simply understanding another language does not mean someone can translate a work of literature. It is a very complex process and it is easy to mis-translate a passage.

MEIN KAMPF

Here is an example of a problem in making any translation. In English we use the word *great* but it has various meanings: large, wonderful, powerful. It is very similar in German. They too have many words with multiple meanings which are often interchangeable, but one meaning is more correct than any of the others. This was a problem in past translations. The translator would pick the most common meaning which may not always be the best meaning and this in turn alters the meaning of the sentence, "God is great." Translated into another language as "God is big" or is it translated to "God is fat" or "God is powerful" or "God is extensive" or "God is very large"? All are possible translations and all are technically correct if you only translate the words, however none of those examples are true to the original meaning of the simple three word sentence.

These kinds of translation problems are found thousands of times when comparing the original German to the older 1930's and 1940's translations. The Ford translators spent a great deal of time and effort to make sure the Ford translation was not only technically correct, but true to the original meaning and intent of Hitler's words.

It was common to use past perfect tense in *Mein Kampf*, and in German writing in general, they would say "the meeting took place" instead of saying "we held a meeting." This can make reading seem slow and boring. Many of these instances were changed to be more active or at least less confusing in the Ford translation. This helps make the Ford translation easier to read.

Comparing Translations

Hitler's original sentences contained multiple clauses and long sentences which pieced together many thoughts in a flow-of-consciousness format. There was originally no editing to make it understandable, not even in the original German version. Many criticize the old translations for being disjointed and rambling. This ignores the fact that Hitler was a speaker and not a writer and he was speaking to the common man. If he had been too eloquent his message would have been rejected and he would have been seen as a member of the polished and proper bourgeois. His message was calculated to capture his audience and he says exactly this in *Mein Kampf*.

We will analyze the various translations and reveal major problems in some versions.

Some problems in older translations are:
- inaccuracy
- biased word choices
- confused translations
- incomprehensible sentences
- alteration of meaning
- misunderstanding of original meaning
- skipping sections that the translator did not understand
- using uncommon and archaic words

- removing style elements of Hitler's speech
- embellishment by the translator
- replacing inciting words with more casual words
- replacing idioms or expressions with inaccurate English versions
- removing idioms or expressions and losing their meaning
- mistranslating idioms
- using unfamiliar names or places without explanation
- misunderstanding references to places or people resulting in incorrect or confusing passages

If one word is changed, it is not always a big deal but when you change a word here and another there, then elaborate in one area but not another, the original style is lost. Hitler's style is important because this style is what listeners heard at his speeches, this is the style that moved them emotionally and made them want to follow him. When the style is lost, Hitler is lost and it becomes a jumble of words.

The Ford Translation

You cannot criticize a work if you cannot read it. You cannot support a work if you cannot understand it. Past translations omitted or softened passages which clearly revealed Hitler's policy and goals. Confusing sentences in older translations, uncommon words, and a poor understanding of the underlying meaning, all combined to obscure the original thoughts Hitler loudly expressed in his prison cell. To truly understand Hitler requires a *Mein Kampf* translation that can be understood by the average person.

More people than ever are discussing *Mein Kampf* on the Internet, but very few of them have actually read it. They assume they know what it contains. Some express opinions without understanding what they are so violently against. Most Nazi sympathizers claim allegiance to the book but cannot quote a single line from it. Neither person can explain why they have strong emotions and a strong point of view because they have no idea what is actually in *Mein Kampf*.

All they can say is that they know *Mein Kampf* is bad or good because they believe that is what they should believe. If you want a reason to dislike or like *Mein Kampf*, then read it. Then you can justify your claims.

The lack of an audio version limited the availability of *Mein Kampf* to the average, busy person. *Mein Kampf* is now available to many more people in an audio format and the Ford translation is the only complete audio version with 30 hours of audio as well as a printed book version.

This version takes into account the many updates and corrections made throughout the printing history of the original German version. There were passages which were made clearer, some were omitted for various reasons (if they were important then they are preserved in this edition, if they were unnecessary restatements they were omitted to match the official version).

The line by line mechanical translations of the past lack the original passion that drove Hitler and swayed the emotions of the German people. The older translations, which were translated in a mechanical way, clearly missed the point of many passages in *Mein Kampf*. They mistranslated references, and even edited out jokes because they failed to realize Hitler was making a joke.

Many sentences were clarified to make them understandable in the Ford translation. A number of original German sentences were written in a shorthand form that is common in speaking but confusing in writing. When we speak, we often make assumptions about the subject of the sentence or even the verb which is perfectly clear with inflection or hand gestures or based on the situation. However, in writing some of these sentences, which were dictated by Hitler, seem to make no sense. Only after careful analysis can their meaning be determined. These shorthand sentences were often omitted in older translations. The translators could not understand what was being said so they left them out. The Ford translation has restored these sentences.

The older translations also included obscure historical references which were not explained. These are explained in the Ford translation. For example, when Hitler says "We will finish what was started 600 years ago!" What does that mean? The old translations do not say and the reader is left confused. The Ford translation includes notes which explain such references. Without this clarification, modern readers would be unable to understand most of the references to people and places, and many other seemingly obscure sayings which had meaning to the people of the time but are uncommon today. Here is the passage from the Ford Translation with the explanation inserted.

> We will begin our work where it was left off six hundred years ago.(*A reference to the Old Prussia of the 13th and 14th century when Teutonic Knights conquered regions and brought in ethnic Germans.*)

Here is another example showing how historical notes make the meaning clearer in the **Ford translation:**

> Therefore finding men from this group who were ready to sacrifice their own lives in the service of the new ideal was Love's Labor Lost, it was impossible. (*Love's Labor Lost is the title of a Shakespeare comedy which came from a Greek poem that says "To do good to one's enemies is love's labor lost" doing good to your enemies is futile, and here is meant as an expression of futility.*)

You can see how the note in parentheses helps the reader understands the reference. Some of the older translations did not recognize the reference and translated in such a way that the phrase "Love's labor lost" was not even included. Without this explanation most people would have no idea what the reference was. Even if they looked it up, they would still not know what it meant. This is an example of how the Ford translation has improved the understandability of *Mein Kampf.* Also notice how the Ford translation not only used the phrase correctly, but it includes a plain English version ("it was impossible") right in the sentence to make it extra clear what is being said.

The older translations included many obscure references to names and places such as the following example. In older translations the name Dorten is not identified except to give his last name. Any average reader would have no idea who this refers to or what it means in context. The Ford translation gives a full account of such references to make the text clear. This is not just a generic historic reference where the person's name is listed with their birth/death and a few words about them. No, the Ford translation includes a complete description AS IT APPLIES TO THE REFERENCE. That means that you are not given generic information but specific information that explains what the reference means in the sentence where it us used.

Many of these references were well known at the time but have faded into history. Most Readers of 1927 knew what they meant, but their names are unknown to modern readers, even in Germany. Here is the passage from the Ford translation with an explanation that

MEIN KAMPF

matches the context:

> I considered and still consider those organizers to be traitors even to this day. They were hired and paid for by France. In the case of Dorten, history has already passed judgment. (*Hans Adam Dorten, attempted a non-violent putsch in the German city of Mainz which was unsuccessful and resulted in an arrest warrant for treason. He took refuge in the French occupied Rhineland, the name for the area on both sides of the Rhine river, and formed a political party there supported by the French, however, due to his treason indictment, the other political parties looked down on the new party.*)

You can see how the Ford translation explains who Dorten is plus what the reference in *Mein Kampf* actually refers to.

The Ford translation of *Mein Kampf* opens the work up to a much broader audience. The availability in an audio format also makes it available to more people who want to understand the mind that created the Nazi movement but are unwilling to read such a long book.

Hitlerisms

A Hitlerism means the style used by Hitler. Everyone has certain words, phrases, or sentence structures he personally favors when writing or speaking. Hitler's books were dictated, however his speaking style is clearly present in them.

Much of Hitler's original wording and style was filtered out of past translations, for example when Hitler said "through and through" it was simplistically translated as "through" in older translations. When Hitler said "dragging the nation into an abyss of tears" the older translators changed it to "dragging a whole nation down with itself" or another translation said "drags down the whole nation with it into the abyss." You may think such simple omissions are minor, however when they occur in every second or third sentence, they collectively damage the overall translation, they cut out the original style and flow, making the writing seem stilted and flat. Sometimes these seemingly minor omissions alter the meaning of the passage entirely.

Here is an example of Hitler's sarcastic wit as it comes across in the Ford translation:

> "To hold a strike, the Marxists[union leaders] were needed, since it was primarily the workers who had to strike."

Here, Hitler was talking about a labor strike and obtaining the Marxist's support. At that time the Marxist political movement in Germany controlled the unions therefore the workers. A very sharp piece of wit in a paragraph dripping with sarcasm which has been unknown to English readers of older translations.

It is interesting to note that Hitler spends more time attacking enemies than promoting friends and allies.

Hitler loved to enumerate. Here are five reasons, there are three kinds of people. Most of these enumerations were kept in the Ford translation to preserve his style. Once in *Mein Kampf*, he began counting and forgot to complete the elements of his list. This oversight is highlighted in the Appendix.

Hitler had a tendency to open a discussion with a problem, explain it, and explain it again in the next paragraph. This style is more noticeable in writing and might not be as obvious during a speech. Some people have criticized Hitler for this style, however it is a valid technique when speaking. If you want your audience to remember what you said, you repeat it. This was usually limited to discussing an event, giving an example, veering off of the topic for a sentence or two, maybe a paragraph, then giving another example and discussing the topic some more.

Some people cite where Hitler goes into depth in Volume One about the need for territorial expansion but then again explains it almost word for word in Volume Two as an example of his repeating himself. We must remember that originally Volume One and Two were separate books and only later combined into one book. It is unlikely, if *Mein Kampf* were written as a single book, this duplication would have been included, however it was simply not removed when the volumes were combined.

Mainly in Volume Two, Hitler frequently made references to things already said, such as "As I have already mentioned..." He liked to draw the listener or reader's attention back to what he had previously said. This may have been a method of validating what he was saying as if he were quoting himself as an authority.

Hitler liked to say "mathematical" or "mathematical certainty" too.

Hitler frequently spoke in a long train of thought. This method works in speeches, but in writing it creates complex, long sentences with multiple clauses. Without the vocal inflection to guide the reader, it can be difficult to follow in the original German language.

Hitler often starts a sequence of ideas with "Therefore, the following conclusions result:" "We can, therefore, state the following principles:" or similar introductory statements.

Hitler liked to use "etc." Some older translations edited these out but they are preserved in the Ford translation to keep Hitler's original style. Some people criticize him for using etc. by saying it shows a mind that lacks creativity, however the use of etc. actually indicates a complex thought process that is common in intellectuals who have difficulty making a single statement because their minds automatically attach a long list of possibilities, outcomes, and influences to every thought.

Hitler has a tendency to create multiple top levels. For instance he says an organization's most important goal is to distribute propaganda, then a paragraph later he says the most critical objective of the organization is to select the best people who can carry out propaganda, then a couple of paragraphs later the organization's most important goal is to avoid disagreements between members. This pattern of multiple "most important" considerations is repeated a number of times in *Mein Kampf*.

Hitler used sarcasm heavily in *Mein Kampf*. Because of this, I think it is important to clearly define what we mean by sarcasm.

Contrary to some definitions, sarcasm is not irony used with the intent to wound the person to whom the remark is addressed. Sarcasm can be hurtful intentionally or hurtful for a joke or not hurtful at all. Irony is defined as: *An expression marked by a deliberate contrast between apparent and intended meaning, usually to draw attention to some incongruity or irrationality. A literary style that uses this kind of contrast for humorous or rhetorical effect is also irony.*

These types of irony give a clue to the true definition of an ironic statement. An ironic statement must appear as if you are sincere, there must be no hint of sarcasm, and you must not be aware that the remark is droll. The line must be delivered straight, so that the recipient misses the hidden message, but onlookers get it loud and clear. This was not

MEIN KAMPF

Hitler's style. He made sure everyone knew what he meant by his tone, or quotes in the text. The type of sarcasm Hitler uses was saying the opposite of what was said in words, sometimes to comedic effect. It is the use of words to mean the opposite of what is said.

Hitler often uses a Socratic type of irony which borders on sarcasm because it has attention drawn to it to make it clear. This meant lower classes could easily identify and understand what was really being said. It is the same theory behind good writing. You do not tell the audience everything but give them enough to figure it out for themselves. Yet, at the same time, you cannot make the puzzle too difficult to figure out. It was a technique Hitler used to maintain interest in his speeches and to make people accept what he was telling them as factual. It seemed more valid to the listeners because the audience was able to figure it out.

Sarcasm is often described as the lowest form of wit, but that is incorrect. It is parody that takes that position. Quips are often confused with sarcasm even by the user. They think they are making remarks which are intelligent and sarcastic when in fact they are ignorant and quippy. A quip is a way of indirectly expressing aggression towards others.

The humor of complexity shields the speaker from vulnerability related to openly stating an opinion and standing behind it. "What a great car" can be a quip if the car is clearly not a nice one, but this is not sarcastic. Quip'ers only show a superficial part of themselves and avoid expressing deep opinions as opinions. Users of sarcasm want to make their opinions very clear through their vocal tone(shown by "quotes" in the text of *Mein Kampf*). Sarcasm, true sarcasm, as used by Hitler, is a sign of intelligence and is used to express anger and aggression towards what he sees as unfair, dishonest, or deceiving elements. Sarcasm is highly appropriate in its expressiveness for him.

Spitting out an insult would not have the same effect as the targeted use of sarcasm which combines a jab plus humor which makes a more entertaining statement than the merely negative one would be and it also leads his audience to accept his conclusion and allows them to feel smart because they can figure out what he is saying even though he is not absolutely literal. Sarcasm can also stimulate the ego of the user by asserting themselves as intelligent and powerful. Heavy users of sarcasm are usually aggressive on some level, more than the average person. This can be part of a power game which makes the user feel powerful and can make followers view them as intelligent and powerful which makes them want to follow.

Quips put people down, sarcasm does not, it expresses a hidden opinion in a blatant fashion as if it is a shared secret between the speaker and the listener. It made his speeches more interesting and attractive.

The idea that less intelligent people do not get sarcasm is only partly true. If they are unable to understand sarcasm, then they lack the ability to understand deep meaning anyway. Hitler's use of sarcasm most likely attracted lower educated elements of the population because they could listen and say "yeah, I get what he is saying, what he is really saying."

Hitler's use of sarcasm was to illustrate a point by saying the opposite which could be construed as aggressive in most cases based on his usage. His use of sarcasm is very specific and focused.

German Race References Explained

What did Hitler really say? This is important when understanding his writing. Many people assume Hitler's speeches were hate filled, vulgar episodes comparable to speeches by Neo-Nazi's or the Ku Klux Klan. In fact, Hitler was careful about his public language. He would likely criticize such offensive speeches if he heard one today as being inappropriate for propaganda purposes. He was almost scientifically clean in a way. The words he used were common in his day and were, in themselves, not excessively offensive. The terms Jew and negro merely described a race of people. They were in common use and had no negative associations in themselves. He did not use more charged terms which were available.

The word Hitler used the most was "völkisch" which means 'belonging to a certain race/people'.

Its actual meaning can be more positive or more negative based on context. The word itself sounds very "nice" and "innocent" which is why the Nazis kept using it instead of the racist sounding "rassisch" for a race. The best translation for "völkisch" is one that is somewhat neutral like racialist however it would not be correct to translate it as racist.

'Folkish', 'Populist' and 'Racial' are pretty much interchangeable, however no one uses folkish or populist in common speech. These were commonly used in older translations from the 1930's which obscured the true meaning. If you look up populist or folkish in the dictionary, you will find a very *nice* definition which is not necessarily related to the race-oriented meaning in *Mein Kampf*.

The word ethnic may be considered too religious of a term in German. The German equivalent, ethnisch, wasn't used in the original German texts of *Mein Kampf*. It's used differently and not an accurate translation for völkisch.

It would be inappropriate to translate populist as racist. The word racist in English has a negative taint which was not associated with the words populist/folkish. Therefore we must be careful not to blindly substitute racist for populist even though it would be a valid word substitution based strictly on the definition, the meaning is skewed by social perception if we do so.

For these reasons, the words *populist* and *folkish* which were used in earlier translations were not used in the new Ford translation. The words simply have no modern meaning to the average person. Ethnic is not accurate either so race/racial was the best choice and is the most accurate translation. Populist was most often replaced with race-aware or racialist

MEIN KAMPF

(one who uses race to make decisions or studies racial matters, usually informally) in the Ford translation.

Here are some examples of the actual use of race terms in *Mein Kampf*:

> **Original German:** Sie hat weder das Siedlungsgebiet der deutschen Rasse vergrößert, noch hat sie den – wenn auch verbrecherischen – Versuch unternommen, durch den Einsatz von **schwarzem Blut** eine Machtstärkung des Reiches herbeizuführen.
>
> **Ford translation:** It did not try to enlarge the territory for settlement by the German race or try to increase the power of the Reich through the use of **black blood**, which would have been a criminal act itself.

In German, both the color black and the race are called "schwarz". In this paragraph, "*schwarzem*" clearly references the race. Note also that here German race is originally *deutschen Rasse*, however it is still neutral in meaning.

"Negro" is best translated from "Neger" in German, and "nigger" would remain "Nigger" in German with the same spelling as in English. "Nigger" is clearly a slur, "Neger" can be neutral, so "schwarz" (the adjective) or "Schwarzer" (the noun) are politically correct. Speaking of "schwarzes Blut" (black blood), however, puts a negative spin on things. Blood is red no matter the skin color, therefore using the term "schwarzes Blut" makes the racist sentiments obvious.

> **Original German:** Ich glaube im Gegenteil, daß, wenn dieses Blut der-einst eingesetzt würde, es ein Verbrechen wäre, den Einsatz für zweihunderttausend Deutsche zu vollziehen, während nebenan über sieben Millionen unter der Fremd-herrschaft schmachten und die Lebensader des deutschen Volkes den Tummelplatz afrikanischer Negerhorden durchläuft.
>
> **Reynal-Hitchcock translation:** ...more than 7,000,000 languish under alien rule and the main artery of the German people flows through the playground of black African hordes.
>
> **Murphy translation:** ... neighbouring Germans are suffering under foreign domination and a vital artery of the German nation has become a playground for hordes of African niggers.
>
> **Stackpole- translation:** ... while close by seven millions are languishing under a foreign regime, and the vital highway of the German people has become the playground of hords of African negroes.[sic-hords]
>
> **Manheim translation:** ...while next door, more than seven millions[sic] languish under foreign domination and the vital artery of the German people runs through the hunting ground of African Negro hordes.
>
> **Ford translation:** On the contrary, I believe that if such blood has to be sacrificed, it would be a crime to do so for two hundred-thousand Germans while next door seven

MEIN KAMPF

million are suffering under a foreign regime and the vital lifeline of the German people has become the playground of hordes of African negroes.

Note [sic] *indicates grammatical and spelling errors in the original Manheim and Stackpole editions.*

Murphy translates Negerhorden as 'Nigger'. The RH-translation uses the much nicer 'black African hordes'. I do not believe Murphy did this to make the translation more appealing because he seems to make these decisions randomly. He may have been influenced by the offensive taint to the word. 'Negerhorden' is extremely derogatory due to the use of 'horden'. Here too, 'Horde' most often means a group of animals, not a group of people. However, it still does not say explicitly nigger so his translation was over the top.

'Lebensader' means 'lifeline' or 'main artery'. The full meaning, therefore, is: "the lifeline of the German people runs through the playground of African negro hordes."

'Neger' was at one time a fairly neutral word in Germany. Today, many consider it derogatory. However, context is very important. The word itself is not blacklisted by the media and is sometimes still used on radio. Unlike "Neger", the term "Nigger" is pejorative regardless of context and definitely considered a slur. In 1927 it was not considered to be as serious of a slur but was still considered offensive.

The word "nigger" does not appear in the original German language text of *Mein Kampf*, not once.

In the original Official Nazi English translation which was published by the Nazi party, Murphy uses the word nigger once as shown here:

> During those months, I felt, for the first time that Fate was dealing adversely with me in keeping me on the fighting-front and in a position where any chance bullet from some nigger's rifle might finish me, ...

However, he did not use it again in the Official Nazi version but it appears three times in the British Houghton Mifflin version which was developed from the Official Nazi notes Murphy made. The word negro, or variations of it, occurs 16 times in the Houghton version and it occurs 17 times in the Nazi version.(negro).

In the Nazi version Murphy translates:

> On the contrary, I believe that if we have to shed German blood once again it would be criminal to do so for the sake of liberating two hundred thousand Germans, when close at hand more than seven million Germans are suffering under a foreign yoke and a life-line of the German nation has become a playground for **hordes of African negroes.**

This does NOT say niggers as it did in his later Houghton-Mifflin translation. The change

37

may have been meant to make the version published in England more controversial because the original word is more akin to negro as used in the Nazi translation and as translated by other translators.

Murphy may have wanted to create some quotable quotes but did not want to fill the book with racist words to the point of making it overly offensive so it might have been a marketing decision too.

> **Original German:** Denn was man im allgemeinen unter diesem Wort verstand, war nur die erzwungene äußerliche Annahme der deutschen Sprache. Es ist aber ein kaum faßlicher Denk-fehler, zu glauben, daß, sagen wir, aus einem Neger oder einem Chinesen ein Germane wird, weil er Deutsch lernt und bereit ist, künftighin die deutsche Sprache zu sprechen und etwa einer deutschen politischen Partei seine Stimme zu geben.

> **Murphy translation:** But it is almost inconceivable how such a mistake could be made as to think that a Nigger or a Chinaman will become a German because he has learned the German language and is willing to speak German for the future, and even to cast his vote for a German political party.

> **Ford translation:** What most people thought the word meant was the forced use of the German language. But it is an almost inconceivable error to believe that a negro or a Chinese can become a native German simply because he learns German and is ready to speak the German language in the future and perhaps to cast his vote for a German political party.

Note how Murphy uses the inflammatory Nigger and slightly offensive Chinaman when the original German text actually said *Neger oder einem Chinesen* which simply means "negro and Chinese" and was not a racial slur. Murphy was making the original text more sensational than it actually was.

Neither of them can be considered slurs in this case, especially not "Chinesen" which is a perfectly acceptable description. "Nigger" is clearly too much of a deviation which leaves "negro" as the best translation. The only racial slur for Chinese that is common in German is Schlitzauge which is about as offensive as "chink" in English. Therefore, this is not a slur against the Chinese by Hitler and Murphy's translation is way over the top.

Use of derogatory Kike

> **Original German:** Sowie man nur vorsichtig in eine solche Geschwulst hineinschnitt, fand man, wie die Made im faulenden Leibe, oft ganz geblendet vom plötzlichen Lichte, ein **Jüdlein**.

INACCURATE

> **Murphy translation:** On putting the probing knife carefully to that kind of abscess one immediately discovered, like a maggot in a putrescent body, a **little Jew** who was often blinded by the sudden light.

38

Reynal-Hitchcock translation: When carefully cutting open such a growth, one could find a **little Jew**, blinded by the sudden light, like a maggot in a rotting corpse.

CORRECT

Ford translation: If you carefully punctured this abscess with a knife, like a maggot in a rotten body, who was blinded by the sudden influx of light, you would discover a **Kike**.

This is an example of the only time Hitler used the derogatory word *Jüdlein* in *Mein Kampf*. It is the equivalent of *Kike* in English. Other instances used *Judentum Juden* or variations which are the equivalent of Jew or Jewish. Hitler also made a point of ending the sentence with this slur which was important to preserve his style. Murphy and Reynal changed the word order substantially. Notice how Murphy misunderstood and thought it meant little-Jew and so did Reynal, however little Jew would have been *kleiner Jude* in German.

Hitler avoided racist statements and racist words except for one exception in his entire book.

Words and Grammar

Older translations from the 1930's and 40's were filled with words that were over the heads of the average reader and historical references that were over the heads of the original translators. They had no idea what many references meant so they simply did not explain them. When a reader cannot understand a reference to a person, place, or myth it destroys the modern reader's ability to understand what he is reading. When a modern reader sees a reference to Hecuba he has no idea what it means. The modern reader is just as lost when thrown a word that has changed in meaning over time.

Here is a small example of the unusual words used in the Manheim, Murphy, Reynal Hitchcock, and Stackpole translations:

> hegemony fructified fetters rapidity propitious milliards recalcitrant ineluctable equanimity extirpated chimerical puerile peregrinate sagacity panegyrics vicissitudes freest inter-alia loquacious suavity perfidious preen gasconaders imprecations politicizing comity politicasters upbraided discountenanced redound exhortations vicissitudes honestest evanesce sinecure probity formularies foregathered confraternity elan repudiate particularist effete milliards anathema fatuous intermezzo heretofore suflice autarchic hegemony ignoble, duffers, poltroon, analphabetic vasiclating odious coxcomb sagacity illimitable loquacious conventicles serried ultramontane alacrity ructions

I will take my hat off to anyone who can make a sensible sentence using three of those words without looking them up in a dictionary.

People often have a habit of assuming a meaning for a word when they encounter an unfamiliar word. They may simply blank out or guess at the meaning. Simply assuming a meaning for these words is not adequate for the reader. Many words have subtle meanings and assuming a general meaning for a word because it looks like another does not truly give you an understanding of the material and you certainly do not fully understand the entire book when you encounter such complex and uncommon words on every page. Keeping a dictionary handy is also a poor solution because in the old translations you will find you need it constantly and by the time you comprehend the meaning of a word you may have forgotten what the passage was saying so you end up re-reading every paragraph twice and what is worse, the older translators often picked the wrong word in their translations. They frequently chose the most common definition using their German-English reference and not the most accurate word.

Fortunately, this uncommon word problem was solved with the release of the Ford translation which did away with complex words and replaced them with more common words or with equivalent phrases which were easier to understand and often clearer than the original German word.

Many of the older translations used a strange writing style which put most of the text in a past-perfect or past tense. Even though the original German was like this, it makes the text confusing. The active voice is always preferred in writing. Here is an example where Stackpole used past-perfect:

> **Stackpole translation:** ...primarily those parties were to blame which during the war had refused to think of the Reich.

Here it is in a normal active voice:

> **Ford translation:** As far as Bavaria is concerned, those political parties that put their selfish interests first during the war, ahead of the Reich, were primarily to blame.

It is very disconcerting to read a paragraph, much less a book entirely written in past perfect tense.

Though not as bad, Reynal and Murphy both included an excessive number of past perfect sentences.

Another example:

> **Stackpole translation:** That our people are not used to thinking in terms of foreign policy can be seen best by reading the current press reports concerning the more or less great "love of Germany" on the part of this or that foreign statesman.

Notice how it says "That our people..." instead of simply saying "Our people" and it says "can be seen best by" instead of a more active and simpler "shown by" or "we can see".

Murphy did not use past perfect as often but was often passive.

> **Murphy translation:** The Republic has given to itself the character of an intermezzo in German history.

It could have been better said as: "The Republic created the character of an intermezzo in German history for itself. " Note the passive term "has given".

Different word choices can affect the meaning.

> **Original German:** So sehr wir heute auch alle die Notwendigkeit einer *Auseinandersetzung* mit Frankreich erkennen, so wirkungs-los bliebe sie in der großen Linie, wenn sich in ihr unser außenpolitisches Ziel erschöpfen würde.

> **Murphy translation:** To-day we are all convinced of the necessity of **regulating** our situation in regard to France; ...

> **Stackpole translation:** As much as we all recognize the necessity of a **settlement** with France...

> **Ford translation:** We all recognize that a **confrontation** with France is necessary, however, ...

The German word is *Auseinandersetzung* which means contention, dispute, argument or quarrel. Here we see how Murphy and Stackpole chose softer terms. The original German meant *confrontation*, not regulating or settlement. The Ford translation is the most accurate.

Older translations used terms like military credits to mean military funding or budget which are clearer. Some translate as *military franchise* which should have been translated as *right of soldiers to vote*. Today Franchise means something different. No one would think of it as a voting term today.

Some translators could not understand passages that were very short. They would then guess at the meaning or try to translate them literally. In German they had meaning but in English the meaning is lost unless the translator truly understands the material.

MEIN KAMPF

INACCURATE

Reynal-Hitchcock translation: In the best of faith they acted thus.
Murphy translation: In doing this they acted in perfect good faith.

CORRECT

Ford translation: They did this with the best of intentions.

You can see from the above that the older translations did not understand the meaning of the passage so they translated directly or guessed at the meaning. Here Hitler used a common saying which exists in both German and English, "They did this with the best of intentions.", but neither translator realized what was actually being said.

Many of the older translations used a large number of unneeded words, like basic, also, for instance, so, thusly, generally, the fact that, thus, however, usually, more and more, practical.

It was common to find translated and original sentences with extra words like these.

The parliament took a basic vote...
It is ,also, true that...
For instance,....
Thusly,....

There were many confusing pronouns in past translations, for example a sentence might say "They took up arms against the people but they revolted". Who revolted? The people who were under attack or the ones who took up arms? It is unclear here. This is a common problem in past translations which makes them difficult to understand, ambiguous, and often wrong.

Here is an example of a bizarrely long sentence which was common in the older translations:

Reynal-Hitchcock translation: There I held the viewpoint that, as long as a change in the attitude of the employer towards the employee does not take place, either by measures on the part of the State (which, however, are unfruitful in most cases) or by a general, new education, the only thing the worker can do is to guard personally his interests, by emphasizing his right as an equally important contracting party in economic life; I have further emphasized that such a safeguarding absolutely corresponds to the meaning of an entire national community if through it social injustices, which later are bound to lead to serious injuries of the entire community life of a people, can be prevented; I further declared that this necessity must be considered as existing as long as there are among the employers people who themselves have not only no sense for social duties, but not even for the most primitive human rights; and from this I drew the conclusion that, once such self-defense is considered necessary, its form can sensibly exist only in an integration of the employees on the basis of a trade union.

In the Ford translation it is broken into readable single sentences which make the meaning much clearer and makes it easier to follow.

It is not an error, but it will help you to know the German word putsch means a coup d'etat or a sudden, often violent or forced overthrow of the existing government.

Errors in *Mein Kampf*

We wanted to document all of the errors in past translations, however, we eventually we had to give up. At some points we were documenting three or four errors in a single paragraph which interfered with the task of the translation itself. Also comparing to all older translations became tedious and slowed the process down considerably. The errors in the appendix are only a small part of the thousands of errors found and corrected from each of the older translations.

This error list is by no means comprehensive. We have chosen enough examples to prove the points being made and listed a large enough pool to clearly show that there is a massive problem with older translations. However, there is no way that we could have listed every single translation error from all of the old versions. If we tried, we would basically reproduce the old versions with notes following every paragraph.

Conclusion

What separates *Mein Kampf* from other books on political theory is the simple fact that Hitler did it! He used his formula to take political control of an entire country. His use of the democratic process proved more successful than his attempt at forceful takeover. This clearly separates his writing from the thousands of theoretical political papers and weekend intellectuals posting on blogs.

Other books theorize about how it happened, Hitler tells how he plans to make it happen. He gives details that no theoretician could dream about such as how to setup your political organization, how to choose people for your organization and most importantly who you should not include.

When you finish reading *Mein Kampf*, you will not think Hitler is a nice guy, but you will understand his strength of Will, determination and you will understand how a nation followed him to destruction. You will have a greater understanding of events in the world today and you will understand yourself better as you are forced to ask hard questions during your reading.

What you have received is a true, honest analysis of Hitler's work. This is not an analyses of what it means, what is right or wrong about it, only the written work itself.

I am sure people will read these analyses and decide for themselves that the book is filled with hate without bothering to actually read *Mein Kampf* for themselves. While others will see this analysis as making excuses for Hitler's actions (ignoring the fact that the comments do no such thing and I never analyzed his actions during the war, only his political writings BEFORE the war). Yet others will think the comments do not go far enough. They will focus on the comments that resonate with their own personalities and ignore the rest. That is human nature. Those filled with hate will slam their fist on the table as they proclaim *Mein Kampf* is a work of hate. Those filled with fear will sit back in their chair and announce any analysis did not go far enough in revealing the messages in it. Those who most loudly yell this analysis makes excuses for or justifies Hitler's actions are actually, deep down, themselves sympathetic with Hitler's goals and want to misdirect the people around them by pretending to be against him because they think that is the *correct* way to act. When a person is able to be honest with himself, only then can he objectively look at this work and understand the messages, lessons, and warnings it truly contains.

The majority of *Mein Kampf* discusses politics and conditions in Germany at the time as well as Hitler's building of the Party which is more interesting than it sounds, especially if you have an interest in politics or want to build a business. He also explains, at least he explains what he wants others to believe, his developing anti-Semitism and his feelings about the Jews.

What is important is that the book makes you think about your own opinions, where they

MEIN KAMPF

come from, how you are influenced by the people around you, what choices you make and whether you take action or sit back and let things happen.

Now that you understand *Mein Kampf*, you should pick up a copy of the Ford translation, either the printed book or the audio version, and read or listen to it.

You will find much more food for thought now that you have a stronger understanding of the material in it.

You can find the new Ford translation of *Mein Kampf* at

    www.Mein-Kampf-Audio.com

And you can download a number of free *Mein Kampf* analysis books and commentaries at

    www.HitlerLibrary.org

Find out what it really is about. Then you can decide for yourself.

MEIN KAMPF

Appendix A – *Mein Kampf* Errors & Corrections

Translating from one language to another is very tricky. It is rare to find someone who is equally proficient in both languages. When translating a work that was written in the past, it becomes more difficult because language changes over time. It would be impossible to claim one translation was the only translation. It is possible to show that one translation is better than another. One translator may translate some parts better and not others. A different translator with a different background may interpret passages completely differently resulting in a translation that does not represent the intent of the original author. The Ford translation has attempted to make *Mein Kampf* easier to read while also correcting errors and making the English translation as close to Hitler's intended message as possible.

This appendix documents a small portion of the errors found in various translations of *Mein Kampf*. We began documenting errors as they were encountered but the process of documentation soon became overwhelming. Sometimes we were finding three or more errors in every paragraph of the old translations. Soon we were spending more time documenting errors than translating and verifying. We had to give up the effort to document all errors, and focused on examples that affected the meaning or altered the intent of the passage. Following are the errors found in older translations along with notes explaining the work more deeply.

<u>Card Game</u>

Original German: Genau so kümmerlich sind die Hoffnungen auf den sagenhaften Aufstand im Ägypten. Der „Heilige Krieg" kann unseren deutschen **Schafkopfspielern** das angenehme Gru-seln beibringen, daß jetzt andere für uns zu verbluten bereit sind...

INACCURATE

>**Reynal-Hitchcock translation:** The 'Holy War' can produce in our German muttonheads the pleasant thrill that now others are ready to shed their blood for us...
>**Manheim translation:** The 'Holy War' can give our German Schafkopf players the pleasant thrill of thinking that now perhaps others are ready to shed their blood for us...
>**Murphy translation:** The 'Holy War' may bring the pleasing illusion to our German nincompoops that others are now ready to shed their blood for them.

CORRECT

>**Ford translation:** The promise of a "Holy War" gives a strange, yet pleasant sensation to our German sheeps-head players when they think others are now willing to shed their blood for us.(*Schafkopf or Sheepshead is a card game common in Bavaria*)

>>Manheim most likely left the word untranslated because he did not know what it meant. Manheim did this frequently. If he did not understand a word or passage, he left it as the original untranslated German word or

MEIN KAMPF

phrase and it was up to the reader to figure it out. The Reynal Hitchcock and Murphy translations did not understand the meaning of the word and tried to make Sheeps-Head the game into muttonhead or nincompoops thinking the word meant an idiot. That was not the meaning of Sheeps-Head which is a well known card game. The Ford translation explains the word Schafkopf and lets you know it is a card game. Hitler was talking about men who sat around a table talking and wasting time playing a game, a card game which in itself has no real risk. It might be compared to people today who sit in a coffee shop and talk about politics. They have no idea what they are talking about, but they take great satisfaction in being able to discuss important political matters as if they did know something about them. They do nothing but talk and are happy when they do not have to take any action and others take the risks for them. In Hitler's case there was also the deeper meaning to the reference which is completely lost in the older translations.

The original word Schafkopfrennen is sheep's-head, German-Original: Schaf = sheep, Kopf = head. Schafkopf is a Bavarian card game which is also played in the USA. This card game reference was important to the meaning of the passage because the reference was about how the game was played(which most Germans would know), and how one player allows another, his partner like the card game bridge, to sacrifice for him. It was a very politically charged jab with multiple levels of meaning. These levels were lost in older translations which failed to translate the word or misunderstood the reference completely. The translation of nincompoops and mutton head is completely wrong.

Original German: Auch wenn dieser Erfolg zunächst nur von moralischer Wir-Bündnis kung wäre, er würde genügen, Deutschland ein heute kaum zu ahnendes Maß von Bewegungsfreiheit zu geben.

INACCURATE

Reynal-Hitchcock translation: Even if this result had at first only a moral effect, it would suffice to give Germany a degree of freedom of movement which today can hardly be imagined.
Murphy translation: And even though at first this success would have only a moral effect, it would be sufficient to give Germany such liberty of action as we cannot now imagine.
Manheim translation: Even if this success is limited at first to moral effect, it would suffice to give Germany freedom of movement to an extend which today is scarcely conceivable.
Stackpole translation: Even though this success would at first only have a moral result, it would suffice to give to Germany today a hardly imaginable amount of freedom of action.

47

MEIN KAMPF

CORRECT

Ford translation: Even though this success would initially only have a psychological result rather than a physical result, it would be enough to give Germany today an unimaginable amount of freedom to act on its own.

All of the old translations use the literal translation of *moral*. This is technically correct and is what you find in a German-English dictionary, but when reading the sentence it makes no sense. Most people will read over it, and assume they know what the word moral means, then they will subconsciously imply a meaning. That produces an incorrect interpretation because moral is the wrong English word. Moral would most likely be interpreted to be morality or to be a moral of a story, but both interpretations are incorrect and do not agree with Hitler's meaning. The Ford translation shows the correct meaning which was "the effect would be psychological." We must look at the meaning and not the mechanical conversion of a German word to English. If we research the word and look at how it was used in the German language in the 1920's, then the true meaning is obvious. We can also research the word *moralischer* and if you happen to have a better quality German-English dictionary you will see it has more meanings than the most common one used today(moral) such as moral pressure, moral principle, to seek moral high ground, and psychological meaning how someone thinks something is moral. The meaning here is a combination of moral and psychological, but the English word psychological tells the story accurately. The original phrase was more complex and meant the mental effect on the people who would believe it was right and just(morally right) would be stronger than the physical result. The people would feel better about it psychologically than they would gain materially. It could have been explained in more detail if we said "*...success would initially only have a psychological result in the belief that they were morally right rather than a physical result..*", but that is wordy and does not add to the meaning. Therefore, psychological is the correct word and correctly expresses the meaning of the original German more accurately than the word moral in English. In a different sentence moral would be correct but not here.

The Ford translation did not depend on simple word substitution translation methods and looked for the real meaning of the passages and of words, not just words in a dictionary. Just as in English, German words have multiple meanings which are determined by how they are used. Past translators relied on their German-English dictionary and ignored the meaning of the sentences and ignored what Hitler was trying to say and even ignored how people speak in English. In some places older translators mistranslated a passage that was a restatement of an earlier passage(Hitler often repeated himself) they had previously translated correctly.

Original German: Heute, im November 1926, steht sie wieder im gesamten Reiche frei vor uns, stärker und innerlich fester als jemals zuvor.

INACCURATE

> **Murphy translation:** To-day, in November 1926, it is again established throughout the REICH, enjoying full liberty, stronger and internally more compact than ever before.

CORRECT

> **Ford translation:** Today in November 1926, it is free again throughout the entire Reich and is stronger and more solid internally than ever.

>> Murphy says "more compact", but the original German said *more internally stable*. The Ford translation shows the passage correctly translated.

Original German:...erleben, daß sich die größten parlamentarischen Strohköpfe, wirkliche Gevatter Sattlermeister und Handschuhmacher – nicht bloß dem Beruf nach, was gar nichts sagen würde – plötzlich auf das Piedestal des Staatsmannes emporhoben, um von dort herunter dann die kleinen Sterblichen abzukanzeln. Es tat und tut dabei gar nichts zur Sache, daß ein solcher „Staatsmann" zumeist schon im sechsten …

INACCURATE

> **Murphy translation:** Then we saw--and to-day also--the greatest parliamentary nincompoops, really common saddlers and glove-makers--not merely by trade, for that would signify very little--suddenly raised to the rank of statesmen and sermonizing to humble mortals from that pedestal.
> **Manheim translation:** We were treated to the spectacle (as we still are today!) of the greatest parliamentary thick-heads, regular saddlers and glove makers - and not only by profession, which in itself means nothing - suddenly setting themselves on the pedistal of statesmen,...
> **Reynal-Hitchcock translation:** Then we saw (and one can still see it today) the prize parliamentary dunderheads, honest-to-goodness saddlers and glovemakers not simply by profession either, which would in itself mean nothing suddenly elevated to the pedestal of statesmen, thence to talk down to the ordinary mortal.

MEIN KAMPF

CORRECT

Ford translation: At that time, it was likely to happen, and it is still happening today, that the greatest parliamentarians, those simple-minded straw-heads, who actually are members of the glove maker's guild and master saddle makers, that is not to say their profession makes them dunces, it is simply that they have no training or experience in what they are trying to do, they were suddenly elevated to the pedestal of a statesman and allowed to rebuke the ordinary mortals from their lofty heights.

> The earlier translators did not understand what was being said so they translated it directly by basic word substitution. The result was: "which in itself means nothing" and that is not a clear description of what Hitler was trying to say. The original German actually meant that *these parliamentarians were working as saddle makers and glove makers, I mean really that was their job, and now they are trying to run the government, they are idiots because they do not know what they are doing, not because there is necessarily anything inherently dumb about being a saddle maker or glove maker.* The English version needed more words to be clear. Also, Hitler used a term "Strohkopf" which literally means that someone's head is filled with straw. It's a common German term to describe a dim-witted or simple-minded person. The older translations understood this but they omitted the reference to straw. Some of Hitler's references were repeated or tied into later comparisons so it is important to keep such specific references and not blindly replace them with generic terms. The Ford translation preserved both the original wording and included the meaning to make it clear what was being said.

Original German: ...was sie immer waren. Sang-und klanglos zog Herr Cuno zurück zu seinen Schif-fen, Deutschland aber war um eine Erfahrung reicher und um eine große Hoffnung ärmer geworden.

INNACCURATE

Murphy translation: ...the Red hyenas suddenly broke out of the national sheepfold and returned to be what they always had been. Without sounding any drums or trumpets, Herr Cuno returned to his ships.
Stackpole translation: Without much ado Herr Cuno sneaked off to his ships.
Manheim translation: Quietly and ingloriously Herr Cuno retreated to his ships and Germany was richer by one experience and poorer by one great hope.
Reynal-Hitchcock translation: Herr von Cuno quietly stole back to his ships, but Germany had become richer by an experience and poorer by a great hope.

MEIN KAMPF

CORRECT

Ford translation: Without a whimper, Herr Cuno sneaked back to his ships.

The RH-translation simplified the saying by making it *"Cuno quietly went back to his ships"*. Murphy often embellished and does so here by saying *"without sounding any drums or trumpets"*. The original is a German figure of speech that means "without a whimper." A literal translation is "without any [great] ado, un-wept and unsung." It also translates as "quietly". The revised wording "Without a whimper" carries the meaning and intent of the original wording. It can be argued that "quietly" is accurate which it is. However, it is still not the best translation and it is not true to the original wording.

The Stackpole translation, and other translations, often failed to create coherent passages and instead focused on sentences and sometimes only fractions of a sentence. When these sentences were placed together, the result was not quality writing and did not promote understanding.

Here is a generic example: Bobby went to the store. It was cold.

What was cold the weather or the store? In English we can figure out it was the weather. But, when switching between languages, it is not always so clear. Sloppy translations do not tie sentences together and cause meaning to evaporate. Here is an actual Stackpole Translation example:

INACCURATE

Stackpole translation: They all had hoped, though perhaps not openly, but at least secretly, that preparations would be made to make this most brazen invasion of France a turning point in German history. Also in our ranks there were many who placed their trust at least in the army of the Reich.

CORRECT

Ford translation: They all hoped that, if not openly, perhaps at least secretly, preparations would be made to make this bold invasion by France a turning point in German history. Within our own ranks, there were many who placed their trust in the defense forces of the Reich.

The Stackpole Translation throws in the *Also* word and it does not follow the flow of the thought. This is not a petty point of English grammar, it has to do with understanding. You can read these two sentences and understand what they *really* meant with no difficulty.

MEIN KAMPF

But, when you begin reading a book and encounter such mistakes every two or three sentences, some much worse than others, then you collectively lose meaning in the work, you will become confused, and as has happened with older versions of *Mein Kampf*, many people gave up after the first chapter. They gave up not because they lost interest, but they gave up because they became mentally exhausted trying to understand the material. It had unexplained references, improperly placed words, used some words like *OF* in a sentence three or more times and each time it had a different meaning which made the passage confusing. Readers gave up in frustration.

INACCURATE

Reynal-Hitchcock translation: Down to late midsummer many officers, and certainly not the worst, did not sincerely believe in such a disgraceful development.

CORRECT

Ford translation: Up to late mid-Summer, many officers, and not the worst of the lot, could not accept that such a shameful development would be allowed to continue.

You can see how RH's version completely left out the final words which are shown in the Ford Translation. This changed the meaning of the passage.

INACCURATE

Murphy translation: Up to midsummer of that year several officers, who certainly were not the least brave and honourable of their kind, had not really believed that the course of things could take a turn that was so humiliating.
Manheim translation: Down to late midsummer many officers, and they were assuredly not the worst, had at heart not believed in such a discraceful development.

The RH-translation(not shown) says the officers could not "believe in a disgraceful development" which is similar to Murphy and Manheim. We must ask what did they mean. Should the passage be interpreted to say that they did not think it was real, that they did not support it or that they thought it was an illusion? The sentence is ambiguous. This is a good example of what can happen when translators focus on the translation instead of the meaning.

52

MEIN KAMPF

Original German: Als aber der schmähliche Zusammenbruch eintrat und man nach Hinopferung von Milliarden an Vermögen und von vielen Tausenden von jungen Deutschen

INACCURATE

> **Murphy translation:** Millions of German money had been spent in vain and thousands of young Germans had been sacrificed, who were foolish enough to trust in the promises made by the rulers of the REICH.

CORRECT

> **Ford translation:** This was after a fortune of billions had been spent and many thousand young Germans were sacrificed who had been stupid enough to take the promises of the Reich leaders seriously.
>
> Here *Milliarden an Vermögen* means *billions in fortunes* as shown in the corrected Ford translation. The Murphy translation mistranslated as Millions of money which is itself a grammatical error. It should have been Millions of Marks in Murphy's translation, but that too would have been incorrect because the word was Billions not Millions.

Original German: Sie hat weder das Siedlungsgebiet der deutschen Rasse vergrößert, noch hat sie den – wenn auch verbrecherischen – Versuch unternommen, durch den Einsatz von schwarzem Blut eine Machtstärkung des Reiches herbeizuführen.

CORRECT

> **Ford translation:** It did not try to enlarge the territory for settlement by the German race or try to increase the power of the Reich through the use of black blood, which would have been a criminal act itself.
>
> Murphy says black troops and
> RH-translation says black blood,
> Manheim uses black blood.
>
> The German schwarzem Blut translates to black blood, not negro blood.
>
> In German, both the color and the race are called "schwarz". In this paragraph, "schwarzem" clearly references the race.
> "Negro" is best translated as "Neger", and "nigger" would be

53

MEIN KAMPF

"Nigger" in German as well, same spelling as in English. "Nigger" is clearly a slur, "Neger" can be meant neutrally in certain contexts, and "schwarz" (the adjective) or "Schwarzer" (the noun) are politically correct. Speaking of "schwarzes Blut" (black blood), however, puts a negative spin on things. Blood is red no matter the skin color, therefore using the term "schwarzes Blut" makes racist sentiments obvious.

INACCURATE

Stackpole translation: They all had hoped, though perhaps not openly, but at least secretly, that preparations would be made to make this most brazen invasion of France a turning point in German history.

CORRECT

Ford translation: They all hoped that, if not openly, perhaps at least secretly, preparations would be made to make this bold invasion by France a turning point in German history.

> This Stackpole translation says an *invasion of France*. It is not an invasion OF France. It was describing an invasion BY France. Numerous such errors can be found in the Stackpole edition.

Original German: Nur bürgerliche Gemüter konnten sich zur unglaublichen Meinung durchringen, daß der Marxismus jetzt vielleicht ein anderer geworden wäre, und daß die kanaillösen Führerkreaturen des Jahres 1918, die damals zwei Millionen Tote eiskalt mit Füßen traten, um besser in die verschiedenen Regierungsstühle hineinklettern zu können, jetzt im Jahre 1923 plötzlich dem nationalen Gewissen ihren Tribut zu leisten bereit seien.

INACCURATE

Murphy translation: Only bourgeois minds could have arrived at the incredible belief that Marxism had probably become quite a different thing now and that the CANAILLE of ringleaders in 1918, who callously used the bodies of our two million dead as stepping-stones on which they climbed into the various Government positions, would now, in the year 1923, suddenly show themselves ready to pay their tribute to the national conscience.

Reynal-Hitchcock translation: Only bourgeois souls could work their way around to the incredible opinion that Marxism had, perhaps, now become something else, and that the canaille of bosses who in 1918

MEIN KAMPF

coldly trampled over two million corpses, the better to scramble into the various seats of government, were now, in the year 1923, ready to do their bit for the national conscience.

Manheim translation: Only bourgeois minds can arrive at the incredible opinion that Marxism might now have changed, and that the scoundrelly leaders of 1918 who then coldly trampled two million dead underfoot, the better to climb into the various seats of government, now in 1923 were suddenly ready to render their tribute to the national conscience.

CORRECT

Ford translation: Only those from the privileged-class could entertain the outrageous idea that Marxism might now somehow be different from what it was before and that these villainous want-to-be-leaders in 1918, would suddenly be ready to do what was right for the nation in 1923.

> The word "kanaillös" does not actually exist in German. It is a noun to adjective derivation based on the word "Kanaille" which means either "scoundrel" or "rabble". In this case the correct meaning is "scoundrel" which is best translated as "rascally" or "scoundrelly" or something similar therefore villainous is an accurate direct replacement. Manheim was correct with scoundrelly however this is not a real word in English. I can see how he might have used it to preserve Hitler's style of transforming nouns, adjectives or verbs into other parts of speech and wanting to do something similar in English, however he did not preserve Hitler's style in other sentences this way. Murphy's choice of *Canaille* means rabble or masses or riffraff. No one uses the word canaille in English. Canaille was likely chosen because it has a similar base word(replace C with K in German) and the same origin so it is etymologically accurate, but again, I doubt you have ever seen the word before so the average reader would only be confused by it. The Ford translation maintains the original sentence structure as closely as possible while also keeping the meaning as accurate as possible by using villainous and want-to-be-leaders. The original German meant exactly that, not bosses or leaders, they were wanna-be's.

MEIN KAMPF

INACCURATE

> **Reynal-Hitchcock translation:** By such an attitude they wantonly aid from within in undermining and cutting the ground from under our nation's only means of properly standing up for its life necessities.
>
> Note how *wantonly* is one word. This shows how the RH-translation was rushed to press without thorough proofreading.

Original German: Die völkische Bewegung hat nicht der Anwalt anderer Völker, sondern der Vorkämpfer des eigenen Volkes zu sein.

INACCURATE

> **Murphy translation:** The National Movement must not be the advocate for other nations, but the protagonist for its own nation.
> **Stackpole translation:** The race-Nationalist movement must not be the advocate of other states,...
> **Reynal-Hitchcock translation:** The folkish movement must be not the attorney for other nations, but the vanguard fighter of its own.

CORRECT

> **Ford translation:** The race-based Nationalist Movement must not defend the rights of other nations, but act as the spearhead of its own people's rights.

> The German word *Anwalt* means "advocate" or "attorney" and is more clearly stated when it is expanded into the meaning (shown in the Ford translation) and not limited to the definition of the word *lawyer* or *advocate* which is what you see if you look it up in a German-English dictionary. However, the meaning here is very specific. Later sentences make a reference to Germany not being the "police" of other nations which ties in to this statement and fits perfectly. Attorney or advocate was not the original intention. That is not the literal meaning here. The meaning was more general in English. It makes no sense to say Germany is not the attorney of other nations because the single word does not contain the meaning that was intended. The limitations of the single word in English require more elaboration. This is a good example of how some parts of *Mein Kampf* were difficult to understand. In some places simple words have complex meanings and using a simple word sometimes loses the extra meaning.

MEIN KAMPF

In this usage, it sounds like Germany does not handle the litigation and tort matters for other nations. That was not the meaning. The Ford translation is correct and shows that it meant Germany should not enforce the laws or guard the legal interests or protect the borders of other nations which also ties into the later reference as being the police of nations. It has nothing to do with being an attorney, protagonist, or champion, or advocate. Those words were used because the older translators did not understand the meaning of the sentence within the context and translated it literally.

Also "Vorkämpfer" can be translated as "spearhead" more accurately than champion or other words in this context. Murphy left out the race part and changed it to National Movement instead of race-based movement. An interesting choice.

Original German: So wie die alte deutsche Politik zu Unrecht von dynastischen Gesichtspunkten bestimmt wurde, so wenig darf die künftige von völkischen Allerweltsgefühlsduseleien geleitet werden.

INACCURATE

Murphy translation: The new German policy must not follow the sentimentality of cosmopolitan patriotism.
Manheim translation: German policy was improperly determined by dynastic considerations, and the future policy must not be directed by cosmopolitan folkish drivel.
Reynal-Hitchcock translation: Much as the old German policy was improperly determined from dynastic viewpoints, equally little must the future be governed by dreamy folkish cosmopolitanism.

CORRECT

Ford translation: The former German policy mistakenly followed interests of the royal dynasty, however the future should not be guided by such commonplace sickening sentimentalism.

"Allerwelts-" refers to something that is very common and not special at all. "Gefühlsduselei" means "excessive sentimentalism". A decent translation would be "commonplace sickening sentimentalism".

Manheim, RH, and Murphy's use of *Cosmopolitanism* is not

MEIN KAMPF

accurate. It is also curious how Murphy worded "... follow the sentimentality of cosmopolitan patriotism". That is confusing.

Original German: Sie beweist höchstens die Kraft der Eroberer und die Schwäche der Dulder.

INACCURATE

Murphy translation: At most, the possession of such territory is a proof of the strength of the conqueror and the weakness of those who submit to him.
Reynal-Hitchcock translation: It proves at most the might of the conqueror and the weakness of the victim.
Manheim translation: At most it proves the strength of the conqueror and the weakness of the nations.
Stackpole translation: It but proves the power of the conquerers and the weakness of the sufferers.

CORRECT

Ford translation: Gaining this territory only proves the might of the conquerors and the weakness of those who tolerate them.

The German word Dulder technically translates to "sufferer" if it has to be condensed to a single word. However, here the meaning is more specific. "Dulder" has only one meaning: a person who tolerates something. Here is a paraphrase of the full sentence: "At most it proves the conquerors' strength and the weakness of those who endure them." The Ford translation is the most accurate.

Manheim mistranslated the passage by using the word *nations* which is not the meaning here. It has to do with the weakness of the *people* who were conquered. The other translators used a German-English dictionary to find the suffering meaning but not the real meaning of the passage. Murphy did understand the passage, but he stated by literally translating the German words individually.

The Stackpole edition also misspelled *conquerers* which should be conquerors. Their edition was rushed to press to beat the lawsuit that would stop the sales of their unauthorized edition so it was not proofread well.

MEIN KAMPF

Original German: So wie unsere Vorfahren den Bo-den, auf dem wir heute leben, nicht vom Himmel geschenkt erhielten, sondern durch Lebenseinsatz erkämpfen mußten, so wird auch uns in Zukunft den Boden und damit das Leben für unser Volk keine göttliche Gnade zuweisen, sondern nur die Gewalt eines siegreichen Schwertes.

INACCURATE

Manheim translation: Just as our ancestors did not receive the soil on which we live today as a gift from Heaven, but had to fight for it at the risk of their lives, in the future no folkish grace will win soil for us and hence life for our people, but only the might of a victorious sword.

Reynal-Hitchcock translation: Just as our forefathers did not get the land on which we are living today as a gift from Heaven, but had to conquer it by risking their lives, so no folkish grace but only the might of a triumphant sword will in the future assign us territory, and with it life for our nation.

Murphy translation: The soil on which we now live was not a gift bestowed by Heaven on our forefathers. But they had to conquer it by risking their lives. So also in the future our people will not obtain territory, and therewith the means of existence, as a favour from any other people, but will have to win it by the power of a triumphant sword.

Stackpole translation: ... just as our antecedents did not receive the land upon which we live as a present from Heaven, but had to fight for its possession at the risk of their lives, so also in the future we shall not obtain the land, and with it life for our nation, by any act of grace on the part of the nations, but only by the force of a victorious sword.

CORRECT

Ford translation: Our ancestors did not receive the land we live on as a present from Heaven, but they had to risk their lives and fight for it. In the future, we will not obtain the land, and the life it offers for our nation, through any act of Heavenly generosity. We will only obtain the land we need through the might of the victorious sword.

"Unser Volk" does mean "our people/nation", but the sentence structure is very unusual in the original German.

Here it means: "Just as our ancestors (...), in the future the soil and hence the life for our people will not be allotted by a Divine Grace either*, but by the might of a victorious sword."
*The word *either* refers back to the ancestors who didn't receive their soil from Heaven **either**.

59

MEIN KAMPF

> The Manheim, Murphy, Stackpole and RH translations all incorrectly said "folkish grace" or "other people" or "nation" because they all thought it was referring to the people which it was not. The sentence was referring back to the previous clause. Only the Ford translation is correct here.
>
> Stackpole also chose the unusual word antecedents, meaning an event or one that precedes another, instead of ancestors.

Original German: Denn kein Volk besitzt auf dieser Erde auch nur einen Quadratmeter Grund und Boden auf höheren Wunsch und laut höherem Recht.

INACCURATE

> **Reynal-Hitchcock translation:** For no nation possesses even a single square kilometer of soil and territory on this earth because of a superior will, let alone a superior right.

CORRECT

> **Ford translation:** .. people on the earth possess even one square meter of land and soil as the result of any heavenly wish or higher right.
>
> Reynal mistranslates meter as kilometer. This is an unusual mistranslation because meter is the same in English as German. Here we have Quadratmeter which is Quadrat-meter, square-meter.

Original German: Es ist hier nicht meine Aufgabe oder auch nur meine Absicht, auf das „Wenn" hinzuweisen, falls das „Aber" nicht gewesen wäre. Wohl empfinde ich es jedoch als unbedingte Not-wendigkeit, den bestehenden Zustand ungeschminkt und nüchtern darzulegen, auf seine beängstigenden Schwächen hinzu-weisen, um wenigstens in den Reihen der nationalsozialisti-schen Bewegung die Einsicht in das Notwendige zu vertiefen.

INACCURATE

> **Murphy translation:** It is not my task nor my intention here to discuss what would have happened if certain conditions had been fulfilled. But I feel it absolutely incumbent on me to show the present conditions in their bare and unadorned reality, insisting on the weakness inherent in them, so that at least in the ranks of the National Socialist Movement

MEIN KAMPF

they should receive the necessary recognition.
Manheim translation: ??????????? MISSING???????????????

CORRECT

Ford translation: It is neither my task nor even my intention to point out the "If" in case the "But" had not been present. I do, however, feel that it is absolutely necessary for us to see the existing conditions as they truly existed, without coloring them, and to point out their terrible weaknesses, if only to deepen the knowledge so the situation may be understood within the ranks of the National-Socialist movement.

> This entire passage was missing from the Manheim translation and was heavily altered in Murphy, likely because the meaning was unclear to the translators. It is a difficult passage to decode from the original German. The Manaheim section should have been at bottom page 643 or top of 644 but it was absent(page numbers may differ in various editions).

Original German: Und selbst Frankreich muß unter diese Staaten gerechnet wer-den. Nicht nur, daß es in immer größerem Umfang aus den farbigen Menschenbeständen seines Riesenreiches das Heer ergänzt, macht es auch rassisch in seiner Vernegerung so rapide Fortschritte, daß man tatsächlich von einer Entstehung eines afrikanischen Staates auf europäischem Boden reden kann.

INACCURATE

Reynal-Hitchcock translation: And even France must be counted among these States. Not only because the colored human stock of its enormous empire supplements its army to an ever greater extent, she is racially making such progress in negrofying herself that one can really speak of the establishment of an African State on European soil.
Murphy translation: Not only because she is adding to the strength of her army in a constantly increasing measure by recruiting coloured troops from the population of her gigantic empire, but also because France is racially becoming more and more negroid, so much so that now one can actually speak of the creation of an African State on European soil.
Manheim translation: And even France must be counted among these states. Not only that she complements her army to an ever-increasing degree from her enormous empire's reservoir of colored humanity, but racially as well, she is making such great progress in negrification that we can actually speak of an African state arising on European soil.

61

MEIN KAMPF

CORRECT

Ford translation: Even France has to be included in these states. Not only does she constantly increase and replenish her army out of the negroid livestock from her enormous Empire, but also, from a racial viewpoint, her infiltration with negro blood is increasing so rapidly that we could call it the creation of an African state on European soil.

It is important to correctly translate racial slurs. If something is a racial slur, then it should not be watered down with a more politically correct word. If it is **not** a racial slur, then it should never be enhanced for dramatic effect because both would corrupt the translation.

"Farbig" is a general term that refers to Asians and Africans (mostly to Africans). By itself, it does not qualify as a slur. However, combined with "Menschenbeständen", the expression receives quite a negative spin. The reason for this is that "Bestand" is typically used in conjunction with animals, i.e. livestock. A full translation for "farbige Menschenbestände" might read "negroid livestock".

Vemegenrung is a neologism(invented word) that doesn't exist in the German language. One might translate it as "Negroisation". Hitler did invent several of his own words in his speeches and in *Mein Kampf*.

None of the older translations catch the livestock reference and translate it more nicely as people. Reynal almost gets it by saying *stock* but there is a big difference between calling a group of people stock and livestock. Manheim chooses reservoir which does not have the same meaning as livestock. The new Ford translation uses the correct phrase of livestock and an expanded version of negroisation for clarity.

Original German:...Dienst dieser einzigen großen Mission gestellt werden, bis daß das Angstgebet unserer heutigen Vereinspatrioten „Herr, mach uns frei!" ...

INACCURATE

Reynal-Hitchcock translation:...until the prayer of fear of our present-day parlor patriots,'...
Murphy translation: in the service of this one great mission, until the faint-hearted cry, "Lord, deliver us,"

62

MEIN KAMPF

Stackpole translation: be pressed into the service of this one great mission, until the prayer of fear of our present club-patriots: "Lord, make us free!"

Manheim translation: ...until the timorous prayer of our present parlor patriots: 'Lord, make us free!'...

CORRECT

Ford translation: In this way, the fear stricken prayers of our patriotic social clubs, "Lord, make us free!"

> The original German word is Angstgebet which is Angst-gebet or Angst-prayer or Angst filled prayer, not the single word of fear. Manheim left out the confusing part of the translation and left it as prayer alone. Murphy changed the meaning to faint-hearted cry which has a completely different meaning from the original German. The true meaning is "Fear-stricken prayer" or "prayer of anxiety" or "prayer filled with anxiety".

Original German: Da gerade diese Kreise heute beginnen, die Zielrichtung unserer Außenpolitik in der unseligsten Weise von einer wirklichen Vertretung völkischer Interessen unseres Volkes abzudrehen, um sie statt dessen in den Dienst ihrer phantastischen Ideologie zu stellen,...

INACCURATE

Murphy translation: It is just this circle which is beginning to-day to divert our foreign policy into most disastrous directions and turn it away from the task of promoting the real interests of the nation.

Reynal-Hitchcock translation: Since just these circles are now starting to switch the direction of our foreign policy in the most fatal way from a real advocacy of folkish interests of our people,...

Manheim translation: Since these very circles are beginning today to divert the tendency of our foreign policy in the most catastrophic way from any real defense of the folkish interests of our people...

CORRECT

Ford translation: Today, these very groups are starting a dangerous trend by diverting our foreign policy from a true representation of the racial interests of our people so that it can instead serve their ideology and make their "fantastic" dream come true. Because of this, I feel it is necessary for me to discuss with my supporters as completely and

63

MEIN KAMPF

clearly as possible the most important question of foreign policy and that is our relationship with Russia.

> You can see how the original German word was völkischer which, when used by Hitler, means race or ethnic usually. In the older translations they called it *popular* or *folkish*. Now we must ask what folkish means? What does popular or populist mean? What is more important is to determine what Hitler meant. These are words that change depending on who you ask to define them. They are unclear. Only the Ford translation has the real meaning clearly spelled out as "racial interests" which fits best here. That *is* what Hitler meant and what he said, but past translations did not *get* it. Murphy avoids the racial aspect completely and calls it "real interests" but the word real is not even in the German wording. Again, a clear misinterpretation and alteration of Hitler's words and meaning.

Original German: Als Nationalsozialisten können wir weiter über das Wesen der Außenpolitik eines völkischen Staates folgenden Satz aufstellen:
Die Außenpolitik des völkischen Staates hat die Existenz der durch den Staat zu-sammengefaßten Rasse auf diesem Plane-ten sicherzustellen, indem sie zwischen der Zahl und dem Wachstum des Volkes einerseits und der Größe und Güte des Grund und Bodens andererseits ein gesun-des, lebensfähiges, natürliches Verhält-nis schafft.

INACCURATE

> **Murphy translation:** Moreover, as National Socialists, we must lay down the following axiom regarding the manner in which the foreign policy of a People's State should be conducted: The foreign policy of a People's State must first of all bear in mind the duty of securing the existence...
> **Reynal-Hitchcock translation:** As National Socialists we can further lay down the following principle as to the essence of the foreign policy of a folkish State: The foreign policy of a folkish State is charged with guaranteeing the existence on this planet of the race embraced by the State, by establishing...
> **Manheim translation:** As National Socialists we can, furthermore, establish the following principle concerning the nature of the foreign policy of a folkish state: The foreign policy of the folkish state must safeguard...

MEIN KAMPF

CORRECT

Ford translation: As National-Socialists, we want to make the following statement about the meaning of foreign policy in a racial state. The foreign policy of a racial state has a duty to protect the existence...

> Note the use of the word völkischen which means ethnic state or racial state. Again, the older translations used folkish or peoples-state instead of using the word ethnic or race. By using cleaner words, the true meaning is unclear to the modern reader. The Ford translation matches the original German correctly.

Original German: Nun weiß der Jude zu genau, daß er sin seiner tausendjährigen Anpassung wohl europäische Völker zu unterhöhlen und zu geschlechtslosen Bastarden zu erziehen vermag, allein einem asiatischen Nationalstaat von der Art Japans dieses Schicksal kaum zuzufügen in der Lage wäre.

INACCURATE

Murphy translation: ..he can undermine the existence of European nations by a process of racial bastardization, but that he could ...

Reynal-Hitchcock translation: European peoples and to train them to be sexless bastards, only...

Manheim translation: ...his thousand years of adaptation he may have been able to undermine European peoples and train them to be raceless bastards, but that....

CORRECT

Ford translation: He knows very well that he can undermine European nations and turn them into generic race-less bastards, but he could hardly do the same to an Asian nation such as Japan.

> The terms sexless and racial bastards are not very clear. The original German meant gender-less. Geschlechtslos means genderless/sexless, i.e. neither male nor female. It does not mean neutered. Murphy avoided the translation problem by skipping the word. The word is meant as a substitute for raceless as used by Ford and Manheim because that fits,

65

MEIN KAMPF

however, it is tied to the word bastards which implies a corrupted race by cross breeding, so it would effectively be saying "raceless corrupted race" which does not sound correct. The true meaning is like that of a mannequin, race-less. It may have been Hitler's way of saying robots, i.e. the people will be unthinking undriven robots of a corrupt race that is not a race. This interpretation was used in the Ford translation which used the phrase *generic race-less*. The word was hyphenated to make it easier to read. This passage was not simple to decode. It is open to other interpretations and alternate translations.

Original German: Er vermag heute den Deutschen und den Engländer, Amerikaner und Franzosen zu mimen, zum gelben Asiaten fehlen ihm die Brücken.

INACCURATE

Murphy translation: To-day he can ape the ways of the German and the Englishman, the American and the Frenchman,...
Reynal-Hitchcock translation: Today he can ape Germans and English, Americans and...
Manheim translation: Today he may mimic the German and the Englishman,...

CORRECT

Ford translation: Today, he presents himself like a mime, pretending to be a German, or an Englishman, or an American, or a Frenchman, but he cannot create a bridge to reach the yellow Asian.

The German word is mimen which makes the original word in English *mime*. That makes more sense than ape. Both Murphy and RH translated using the word "ape" which was more common at the time but is not used today in this way. Manheim correctly interpreted the meaning, however he changed the passage by removing the word mime which was the word used by Hitler. This word choice is important because, given Hitler's anti-French attitude, the use of the word had meaning. It was not accidental. Hitler used the word to express a certain lowness or to debase because mimes were considered the lowest of forms of entertainment and they were also French. Using the word mime in itself was an insult that is lost when the word is changed to mimic and confused when changed to ape. You can see that by simply replacing the word a great deal of meaning was lost in the Manheim translation

MEIN KAMPF

even if it may be technically accurate. The Ford translation preserved both the original wording and the meaning. Ape means to mimic to an extreme, often comical or absurd in result. Though the word may have been technically correct, it is not the best choice because it loses Hitler's intended and unspoken twist.

Original German: Für Deutschland jedoch bedeutet die französische Gefahr die Verpflichtung, unter Zurückstellung aller Gefühlsmomente, dem die Hand zu reichen, der, ebenso bedroht wie wir, Frankreichs Herrschgelüste nicht erdulden und ertragen will.

INACCURATE

Murphy translation: As far as concerns Germany, the danger which France represents involves the duty of relegating all sentiment to a subordinate place and extending the hand to those who are threatened with the same menace and who are not willing to suffer or tolerate France's lust for hegemony.
Reynal-Hitchcock translation: For Germany, however, the French danger means an obligation to subordinate all considerations of sentiment, and to
reach out the hand to those who, threatened as much as we are, will not tolerate and bear France's drive toward dominion.
Stackpole translation: For Germany, nevertheless the French danger means the duty to forget all sentimental feelings and to join hands with those
who, just as much menaced as we, are unwilling to suffer and bear France's lust for dominion.
Manheim translation: For Germany, however, the French menace constitutes and obligation to subordinate all considerations of sentiment and hold out a hand to those who, threatened as much as we are, will neither suffer nor tolerate France's desire fo domination.

CORRECT

Ford translation: For Germany, however, the danger posed by the French means we have a duty to forget about bad feelings of the past and join hands with those who are also threatened as long as they are unwilling to suffer or tolerate France's lust for power.

The older translations used the word *sentiment* which is the technical translation of the original German. However, to the

67

MEIN KAMPF

average reader, this passage appears to say "deny sentimental feelings" as if he is speaking of past positive feelings. In English sentiment usually refers to positive feelings or attachments. It makes no sense to deny past positive feelings in order to extend a hand of assistance to someone. Sentiment has a warm and fuzzy feeling to the word and is commonly used to refer to sentimental value, "I feel sentimental about grandma's old hat pin" which is absolutely not the meaning here This is an example of a mechanical translation. The meaning was not to deny-sentiment but to put aside bad feelings from the past.

The original German word, Gefühlsmomente, literally translates to "feeling moments" which the older translations all interpret as sentiment. Technically correct but not correct within the context or original meaning.

Original German: Wer damals nicht mitkämpfte, das waren die parlamen-tarischen Strauchdiebe, dieses gesamte politisierende Partei-gesindel. Im Gegenteil, während wir in der Überzeugung kämpften, daß nur ein siegreicher Ausgang des Krieges allein auch dieses Südtirol dem deutschen Volkstum erhalten würde, haben die Mäuler dieser Ephialtesse gegen diesen Sieg so lange gehetzt und gewühlt, bis endlich der kämpfende Siegfried dem hinterhältigen Dolchstoß erlag. Denn die Erhaltung Südtirols in deutschem Be-sitz war natürlich nicht garantiert durch die verlogenen Brandreden schneidiger Parlamentarier am Wiener Rathausplatz oder vor der Münchener Feldherrnhalle, sondern nur durch die Bataillone der...

INACCURATE

Reynal-Hitchcock translation: Those who did not do their bit then were the parliamentary footpads, the whole politics-playing party mob. On the contrary, while we were fighting in the conviction that only a victorious outcome of the War alone would preserve this South Tyrol to German nationality, the gabblers of these Ephialteses agitated and incited against this victory, until finally the warring Siegfried received a stealthy stab in the back.

Murphy translation: The parliamentary sharpers did not take part in that combat. The whole CANAILLE played party politics. On the other hand, we carried on the fight in the belief that a victorious issue of the War would enable the German nation to keep South Tyrol also; but the loud-mouthed traitor carried on a seditious agitation against such a victorious issue, until the fighting Siegfried succumbed to the dagger plunged in his back.

Manheim translation: ...the ones who did not do their bit at that time

MEIN KAMPF

were the parliamentary sneak-thieves, all the politics-playing party rabble. On the contrary, while we fought in the conviction that only a victorious issue to the War would preserve this South Tyrol for the German nationality, the big-mouths of these Ephialteses agitated and plotted against victory until at the last the battling Siegfried succumbed to the treacherous dagger thrust.

CORRECT

Ford translation: The parliamentary tramps took no part in the fighting. Not this gang of sneaking thieves who spent their time playing party politics instead. On the contrary, while we fought believing that only victory could preserve South Tyrol for the German people, the mouths of these Ephialteses schemed and plotted so long against this victory until finally, the Siegfried yielded to the stab in the back. (Ephialtes was a soldier who betray the Spartan army, he is said to have told the Persians about the pass of Thermopylae around the mountains which they used to attack in the Battle of Thermopylae in 480 B.C. so this reference means a traitor. This reference could also refer to a Greek Ephialtes who made major government changes, taking power away from some, and was assassinated as a result, which would mean a big talker who damages the government in this context. This is the second reference to Ephialtes so it is possible Hitler meant to balance the first mention with a second of a different person as an intellectual joke to see who would understand the second reference of if they would assume it meant the same as the first reference. Siegfried is a German way of saying 'the average Joe' or 'John Smith')

> Murphy omitted the reference to Ephialtes. The other translators included the reference but did not explain what it meant leaving the average reader, who is not a scholar of Ancient Greece, confused.
>
> The word Dolchstoß in German specifically means stab in the back. But, the full expression used is "hinterhältigen Dolchstoß". Therefore, both stab-in-the-back and "treacherous dagger thrust" are good translations. Hitler has previously used it to mean stab in the back specifically and in this sense it is clearly used to imply its meaning as betrayal which is symbolized by stab-in-the-back. Therefore, stab-in-the-back is the most accurate translation.
>
> Footpads is a common German expression for tramp or vagrant and does not literally mean footpads. Murphy mistranslated this word as *sharpers* which is a dishonest person especially a cheating gambler. Manheim mixes up the sentence and calls

them sneak-theives which was actually referring to the second term, but then uses rabble for the second term instead of the first, and Reynal literally translates as footpads, which is of course incorrect in English not to mention comical.

Original German: Unsere jüdische Presse ver-stand es ja immer wieder, den Haß besonders auf England zu konzentrieren, wobei so mancher gute deutsche Gimpel dem Juden bereitwilligst auf die hingehaltene Leimrute flog, vom „Wiedererstarken" einer deutschen Seemacht schwätzte, gegen den Raub unserer Kolonien protestierte, ihre Wiedergewinnung empfahl und somit half, das Material zu liefern, das der jüdische Lump dann seinen Stam-mesgenossen in England zur praktischen propagandistischen Verwertung überweisen konnte.

INACCURATE

Manheim translation: ....German sea power, protested against the rape of our colonies, recommended their reconquest...

CORRECT

Ford translation: They chatted about the "revival" of the German naval power, protested against the plunder of our colonies, and recommended taking them back.

"Rape" can be translated as "Raub" or "Plünderung", but it is more commonly expressed using the sinister contexts of "Schändung" and "Vergewaltigung".
There are a number of places where Hitler uses Raub and there is no clear way to discern which meaning he intended other than the context. It is more commonly used to mean robbery.

The Manheim translation chose the more lascivious and sensational translation of *rape* while Reynal, Murphy, Stackpole Translation, and Ford translations all use the more common *robbery* or *plunder*.

MEIN KAMPF

Original German: Was meine Person betrifft, könnte ich hier bei gutem Gewissen versichern, daß ich soviel Mut noch aufbrächte, um an der Spitze eines zu bildenden parlamentarischen Sturmbataillons, bestehend aus Parlamentsschwätzern und sonstigen Parteiführern sowie verschiedenen Hofräten, an der siegreichen Eroberung Südtirols teilzunehmen. Weiß der Teufel, es sollte mich freuen, wenn einmal über den Häuptern einer derartig „flammenden" Protestkundgebung plötzlich ein paar Schrapnelle auseinandergingen. Ich glaube, wenn ein Fuchs in einen Hühnerstall einbräche, könnte das Gegacker kaum ärger sein und das In-Sicherheit-Brin-gen des einzelnen Federviehs nicht beschleunigter erfolgen als das Ausreißen einer solchen prachtvollen „Protest-vereinigung".

INACCURATE

Reynal-Hitchcock translation: The Devil knows I would be glad if, for once, a couple of shrapnel shells suddenly exploded over the heads of one of those 'fiery' protest rallies. I think the cackling would hardly be more furious or the individual fowls' [Federvieh: poultry or literary gentry; untranslatable pun] dash for safety ensue ...
Murphy translation: Only the Devil knows whether I might have the luck of seeing a few shells suddenly burst over this 'burning' demonstration of protest. I think that if a fox were to break into a poultry yard his presence would not provoke such a helter-skelter and rush to cover as we should witness in the band of 'protesters'.
Stackpole translation: The devil knows I would love it if all of a sudden some shrapnel would burst over the heads of such a "flaming" protest-demonstration. I am convinced that if a fox would break into a fowl-house, the cackling could harly[sic] be worse, and the chicken could hardly run for safety faster than such a "protest-demonstration."
Manheim translation: God knows it would give me pleasure if suddenly a few shrapnel would burst over the heads of such a 'faming' protest demonstration. I think if a fox were to break into a chicken-coop the cackling could hardly be worse, or the rush of the feathered fowl for safety any quicker, than the flight of such a splendid 'protest rally.'

CORRECT

Ford translation: The devil knows I would be glad if, all of a sudden, a shrapnel shell burst over the heads of these demonstrators in this "fiery" protest. I am convinced that if a fox broke into a hen house, the cackling could not be any worse and the chickens could not run for safety any faster than what would occur at this "protest-rally."

- Manheim translates the passage with "God knows" but the original German says the *devil knows*.
- Murphy says *burning* demonstration, but it is more accurately

71

translated as *flaming* and in this specific case it more accurately means *fiery* which means the spirit not actual burning.

Murphy also says "the devil knows whether" but the original text did not give this conditional wording and did not say "whether". The *untranslatable* pun identified by RH in this paragraph was a play on the sound of the words "Federvieh" which simply means poultry. There is no better translation. Here it means a poultry yard but the common English equivalent saying is "*a fox in the hen house*".

RH also says "*the devil knows I would be glad*" which is correct. Neither says "*love*" as in the Stackpole translation; that is too strong. The *harly* misspelling instead of *hardly* is in the original Stackpole translation too. The Ford translation shows the correct wording.

Original German: Genau so wird unser deutscher Pazifist zu jeder auch noch so blutigen Vergewaltigung der Nation, sie mag ruhig von den ärgsten Militärgewalten ausgehen, schweigen, wenn eine Änderung dieses Loses nur durch Widerstand, also Gewalt, zu erreichen wäre, denn dieses würde ja dem Geiste seiner Friedensgesellschaft widersprechen.

INACCURATE

Reynal-Hitchcock translation: In exactly the same way our German pacifist will pass over in silence the most bloody rape of the nation, it may come from even the fiercest military powers, if a change of
Murphy translation: In the same way our German pacifist will remain silent while the nation is groaning under an oppression which is being exercised by a sanguinary military power, when this state of affairs gives rise to active resistance; because such resistance means the employment of physical force, which is against the spirit of the pacifist associations.

CORRECT

Ford translation: In the same way, our German pacifists will ignore the bloody rape upon the nation, no matter how bloody, even if it is carried out by the most evil military forces, if the only way to avert this fate is by resistance and force.

Hitler used the word Vergewaltigung which is more accurately translated as "rape". He only used this word twice in the original German edition.

MEIN KAMPF

> The translation "rape" does not appear in the Murphy translation at all. Here is an example where Murphy cleaned up the translation by simply saying "groaning under an oppression". Reynal, Manheim and the Ford translations used the correct wording.

Original German: Denn ich konnte schon nach kürzester Zeit, ja schon im Verlauf der Aussprache über diesen meinen ersten Vortrag, feststellen, daß die Leute über den Friedensvertrag von Brest-Litowsk in Wirklichkeit gar nichts wußten, daß es aber der geschickten Propaganda ihrer Parteien gelun- gen war, gerade diesen Vertrag als einen der schändlich- sten Vergewaltigungsakte der Welt hinzustellen.

INACCURATE

> **Murphy translation:** For after the discussion which followed my first lecture I quickly ascertained that in reality people knew nothing about the Treaty of Brest-Litowsk and that able party propaganda had succeeded in presenting that Treaty as one of the most scandalous acts of violence in the history of the world.

CORRECT

> **Ford translation:** As I learned from the discussion after my first lecture, people knew nothing whatsoever about the Treaty of Brest-Litovsk, but they had been indoctrinated by their parties' skilled propaganda machine to ridicule this treaty because they were taught it was one of the world's most shameful acts of rape which Germany had committed against Russia.
>
> > Here is another example where Murphy edited out the word rape and chose a less confrontational phrase "scandalous acts of violence". The Ford translation accurately translates the original German based on the context as well as the technical translation.

Original German: Unsere jüdische Presse ver-stand es ja immer wieder, den Haß besonders auf England zu konzentrieren, wobei so mancher gute deutsche Gimpel dem Juden bereitwilligst auf die hingehaltene Leimrute flog, vom „Wiedererstarken" einer deutschen Seemacht schwätzte, gegen den Raub unserer Kolonien protestierte, ihre Wiedergewinnung empfahl und somit half, das Material zu liefern, ...

73

MEIN KAMPF

INACCURATE

Murphy translation: And many of our good German simpletons perch on these branches which the Jews have limed to capture them.
Reynal-Hitchcock translation: Our Jewish press always knows how to concentrate special hate against England, whereby so many good German jackasses have so eagerly crawled into the snare set by the Jews, ...

CORRECT

Ford translation: Then, many good, and stupid, German gimpel(*a German name for the finch, little birds, also meaning one who is so extremely foolish they are saintly*) willingly landed on the sticky twig which was specially pruned by the Jew to capture them.

> Gimpel is the name of a bird (called Bullfinch in English) as well as a pejorative expression for someone short-witted in German. The bird can be caught easily through the use of a Leimrute (lime twig). This twig is also known in German as a "glue trap" and is a sticky twig.
> There was a later, apparently unrelated, story which was published in English in 1957 but may have existed earlier in the original Yiddish or German about the bird. It is unknown if Hitler was referencing this story or not when he referred to a Gimpel as a bird in *Mein Kampf*. The story refers to Isaac Bashevis Singer's Gimple the Fool in Weiss where he is foolish to such an extreme he is saintly and becomes a Wandering Jew, from Jewish, or more accurately Yiddish, Literature.
>
> Murphy omits the bird reference entirely along with the sticky branch reference and cuts it down to "simpletons". He then uses the word "limed" instead of sticky(limed does mean a sticky substance smeared on branches to catch birds, but the average reader would not know that). RH changed the term to "jackasses crawling into the snare", but the original German does not use the word jackass. The Ford translation is the only one that is both accurate and explains the reference in the text.

Original German: Ich muß dabei eines besonderen Steckenpferdes gedenken, das in diesen Jahren der Jude mit außerordentlicher Geschicklichkeit ritt: Südtirol. Jawohl, Südtirol. Wenn ich mich hier an dieser Stelle gerade mit dieser Frage beschäftige, dann nicht zum letzten, um eine Abrechnung zu halten mit jenem allerver-logensten Pack, das, auf die Vergeßlichkeit und Dummheit unserer breiteren Schichten bauend, sich hier anmaßt, eine nationale Empörung zu mimen, die besonders den parla-mentarischen Betrügern ferner liegt als einer Elster redliche Eigentumsbegriffe.

MEIN KAMPF

INACCURATE

Manheim translation: Here I must recall a special hobby which in these years the Jew rode with amazing androitness: the South Tyrol. Yes, South Tyrol. If I here concern myself with this particular question, it is not least to settle accounts with that hypocritical rabble which, counting on the forgetfulness and stupidity of our broad strata, has the insolence to mimic on this point a national indignation, which is more alien especially to the parliamentary swindlers than honest conceptions of property to a magpie.

Reynal-Hitchcock translation: I must recall a special stalking horse which in these years the Jew rode with extraordinary cleverness: South Tyrol. Yes, South Tyrol. Where is our Babbitt in whose spiritual face there does not burn instantly the flame of holy rebellion for this cause? If I take up precisely this question at this point, it is not least of all in order to settle accounts with that most mendacious pack which has arrogated this matter unto itself, building on the forgetfulness and stupidity of our broad layers to fake a national rebellion, which is as especially remote from these parliamentary swindlers as is a respectable conception of property from a magpie.

Stackpole translation: I must mention, moreover, one particular hobby pursued in these years by the Jew with special skill: South Tyrol. On which of the intellectual faces of our philistines does not the flame of utter indignation burn? If I take up this question here at this juncture, I do this in order to settle an account with that mendacious rabble, which, counting upon forgetfulness and the stupidity of the masses of our people, takes it upon itself to fake a national indignation, which these parliamentary rascals possess less than a magpie possesses a conception of the rights of property.
Yes, South Tyrol.

CORRECT

Ford translation: I must mention one particular hobby-horse which the Jew rode with special skill during those years: South Tyrol. Yes sir, South Tyrol.

> The older translations say a *hobby* was ridden. It means a hobby-horse which is a toy horse on rockers that small children play with. The modern meaning for hobby is different when it is used alone which confuses the modern reader who thinks of stamp-collecting, photography or some similar hobby.

75

MEIN KAMPF

Also note how they translated Jawhol as Yes, but Ja is yes in German, Jawhol means more accurately yes-sir. It is also used in the German military in the same way English speaking countries use "yes sir". The older translation of *yes* destroyed Hitler's style of speaking.

The Jawhol is a humming or rolling way of saying Yes, as we in English might say Yeah, Yep, or Yeahhhhh. (Not Yea, that is what you shout when your team scores a goal.)
The use of the word is stronger than a simple Yes as if it is saying a strong. Jawhol is not *Yes*.

Reynal translates hobby as stalking horse instead of hobby-horse.

The Stackpole Translation mistranslated the German word Steckenpferdes by calling it a "hobby" which is literal and is the correct translation, though I do call it a mistranslation because the meaning is lost here. It is German-shorthand for hobby-horse. RH says "cleverness" which does not fit and appears the translator did not understand the sentence.

This section is continued in the same paragraph from the previous example.

Original German: Wenn ich mich hier an dieser Stelle gerade mit dieser Frage beschäftige, dann nicht zum letzten, um eine Abrechnung zu halten mit jenem allerverlogensten Pack, das, auf die Vergeßlichkeit und Dummheit unserer breiteren Schichten bauend, sich hier anmaßt, eine nationale Empörung zu mimen, die besonders den parlamentarischen Betrügern ferner liegt als einer Elster redliche Eigentumsbegriffe.

Manheim translation: Here I must recall a special hobby which in these years the Jew rode with amazing androitness: the South Tyrol. Yes, South Tyrol. If I here concern myself with this particular question, it is not least to settle accounts with that hypocritical rabble which, counting on the forgetfulness and stupidity of our broad strata, has the insolence to mimic on this point a national indignation, which is more alien especially to the parliamentary swindlers than honest conceptions of property to a magpie.

Reynal-Hitchcock translation: I must recall a special stalking horse which in these years the Jew rode with extraordinary cleverness: South Tyrol. Yes, South Tyrol. Where is our Babbitt in whose spiritual face there does not burn instantly the flame of holy rebellion for this cause? If I take up precisely this question at this point, it is not least of all in order to settle accounts with that most mendacious pack which has arrogated this matter unto itself, building on the forgetfulness

MEIN KAMPF

and stupidity of our broad layers to fake a national rebellion, which is as especially remote from these parliamentary swindlers as is a respectable conception of property from a magpie.

Stackpole translation: I must mention, moreover, one particular hobby pursued in these years by the Jew with special skill: South Tyrol. On which of the intellectual faces of our philistines does not the flame of utter indignation burn? If I take up this question here at this juncture, I do this in order to settle an account with that mendacious rabble, which, counting upon forgetfulness and the stupidity of the masses of our people, takes it upon itself to fake a national indignation, which these parliamentary rascals possess less than a magpie possesses a conception of the rights of property.
Yes, South Tyrol.

CORRECT

Ford translation: I must mention one particular hobby-horse which the Jew rode with special skill during those years: South Tyrol. Yeah, South Tyrol.(South Tyrol was part of the Austrian-Hungarian Empire and was annexed by Italy at the end of the First World War including ethnic German areas, Hitler was angry at the loss of the territory, this annexation was not part of the Wilson Fourteen Points Plan for the division of territory but nothing was done to stop it.) Can you not look at any of the faces of our intellectual fools and see the flame of utter indignation burning? If I take up this question here, at this point, I do so in order to settle an account with that most dishonest rabble crowd which counts on the forgetfulness and the stupidity of the masses of our people. This group pretends they are upset over South Tyrol's loss, but the feeling of anger when it comes to abuses of the nation is more foreign to these parliamentary rascals than the idea of property rights is foreign to a magpie.

There is a German saying using the word: Elster (magpie).

German- Die Elster stiehlt, so gut sie schwatzt.
English- The magpie steals as well as it chatters.

Elster or magpie, German common uses of this word mean "always stealing things", "sticky fingers" or "to chatter like a magpie".

RH, Murphy, Stackpole and Manheim translated as "concept of property to a magpie" which is not terrible, but not as good as it could be.
In the second sentence RH says Babbitt(a narrow minded person with a material attachment to bourgeois values), but Murphy says

77

MEIN KAMPF

CANAILLE(the masses or proletariat), Manheim says "hypocritical rabble", and the Stackpole Translation says philistines. That is quite a broad array of interpretations.

From the tone it sounds like Hitler is talking about the bourgeois or leaders, not the proletariat.

The line asking a question is not in Murphy's translation at all. It is in RH's translation. It is not in Manheim's translation. It is in the Stackpole Translation and Ford translation. It appears this line was dropped in later German editions, especially after Volume 1 and 2 were combined. Some translators may not have referenced earlier editions or not felt it was important.

The *faces* line may have been taken out because in the original German, it was simply confusing and hard to understand. "allerverlogenstes Pack" means "most dishonest/mendacious rabble" not Babbitt or Canaille, but those are close.

Original German: Mit Unverstand haben diese Handlungen nichtntioneion mehr zu tun: Denn was jedem denkenden Gehirn eben als undenkbar erschienen wäre, Raubben die geistigen Zyklopen unserer Novemberparteien fertiggebracht: sie buhlten um Frankreichs Gunst.

INACCURATE

Reynal-Hitchcock translation: These actions have nothing at all to do with lack of understanding; for the spiritual centaurs of the November parties contrived everything which would have seemed unthinkable to any thinking brain: they sued like lovers for France's favor.

Murphy translation: Their way of acting cannot be attributed to a want of understande what seemed to every thinking man to be inconceivable was accomplished by the leaders of the November parties with their Cyclopean intellects. They bowed to France and begged her favour.

Stackpole translation: These acts cannot be classified as acts of lack of underbrainstanding. For the mental cyclops of our November parties have done what would appear unconceivable to any thinking brain : they strove for France's favor.

CORRECT

Ford translation: These acts cannot be dismissed as the result of poor understanding. The mental Cyclopses of our November parties have doneis the things that would be inconceivable to anyone who had a working brain.(The Cyclops has one eye, this reference means the parties are functioning on half a brain) They actually solicited France's favor.

RH translates Cyclops incorrectly as centaur which totally changes the symbolism. The original German does say Cyclops or actually Cyclopean which in German is Zyklopen. Stackpole translated this part as underbrainstanding. I have no idea what that was supposed to mean. The original German text translated literally to thinking-minds or thinking-brains so the Stackpole translators apparently made up their own word.

RH mistranslates *buhlten* from German as "sued like lovers". The real meaning is *courted* and in this sense means solicited or sought or *gain the favor of,* but somehow Reynal twisted it into *suing like lovers*. Perhaps they meant "wooing like lovers"? Murphy also over-translated it as begged which is not accurate because the word is too strong when compared to the original German meaning, which as I said, is more along the lines of seek, attract.

The choice of cyclops is interesting because there is a Cyclops freshwater animal that is commonly described as having "cosmopolitan distribution" which could be linked to the previous Jewish references by Hitler about "cosmopolitan" Jews, however he does say Intellect of Cyclops or Cyclopean minds which seems to imply the reference was about the traditional one eyed Cyclops of Greek myth. The sea creature lacks intellect so it is not the reference here, however it may have been a secondary reference since Hitler has previously mentioned such sea life as the polyp.

Thinking brain means a "working mind" or "working brain" as opposed to a non-functional mind.

The reference to Cyclops means they are mental one-eye's or operating on less than full capacity, idiots. This meaning is completely lost in the RH-translation which mistranslates to centaurs.

MEIN KAMPF

An example of Murphy's creative embellishment:

Original German: Wer sich die Mühe nimmt, heute rückblickend die außen-politische Leitung Deutschlands seit der Revolution zu verfolgen, der wird nicht anders können, als sich angesichts des fortwährenden unfaßbaren Versagens unserer Regierungen an den Kopf zu greifen, um entweder einfach zu verzagen oder in flammender Empörung einem solchen Regi-ment den Kampf anzusagen.

INACCURATE

> **Murphy translation:** If we take the trouble to cast a glance backwards on the way in which German foreign policy has been conducted since the Revolution we must, in view of the constant and incomprehensible acts of submission on the part. of our governments, either lose heart or become fired with rage and take up the cudgels against such a regime.

CORRECT

> **Ford translation:** If we bother to look back at Germany's foreign policy after the Revolution, we are shocked by the constant failures of our government. A man who sees the constant and incomprehensible decline of his government can only drop his head in despair, or feel the beginning of an internal desire for a flaming rebellion against such a regime.

> The Murphy translation shows some of his creative writing skills by adding the reference to taking-up-cudgels which is not in the original German text. The true meaning as shown in the Ford translation is simply flaming indignation and it says nothing about cudgels.

Original German: Frankreich und Rußland allein boten jeder übermäßigen Entwicklung deutscher Größe Hindernisse und Widerstand. Die außerordentlich ungünstige militärgeographische Lage des Reiches konnte als weiterer Sicherheitskoeffizient gegen eine zu große Machtzunahme dieses Landes gelten.

INACCURATE

> **Murphy translation:** France and Russia alone hindered and opposed the excessive aggrandizement of Germany.
> **Reynal-Hitchcock translation:** By themselves, France and Russia offered obstacles and resistance to every disproportionate development of German stature.

MEIN KAMPF

CORRECT

Ford translation: France and Russia were the only countries who placed obstacles in Germany's path and excessively resisted the development of Germany's expansion.

Murphy translated the passage as "excessive aggrandizement" which is not consistent with the writing of Hitler. Hitler would never have characterized Germany's expansion as "excessive".
Reynal also gave an inappropriate translation by using the word "disproportionate" which Hitler clearly would not have used because he wanted Germany to expand and believed it was Germany's God given right to do so, therefore he would never have described expansion as excessive or disproportionate.
The literal translation was: *France and Russia alone offered excessive resistance obstacles to development of German's size.* Here you can see that the intended meaning is not that Germany's desire to expand was excessive, which is not a logical thing for Hitler to say, but that France and Russia were excessive when they resisted Germany's efforts to take land they occupied.
Both old translations missed the reference to Germany's size expansion and none included the reference to size which was important to the passage in order to understand it. RH took it to mean stature as in social-status among countries, and Murphy used the odd word of aggrandizement which is simply inaccurate. The Ford translation is more true to the meaning.

Original German: Dieses Schwert zu schmieden, ist die Aufgabe der innerpolitischen Leitung eines Volkes; die Schmiedearbeit zu sichern und Waffengenossen zu suchen, die Aufgabe der außenpolitischen.

INACCURATE

Murphy translation: The forging of this sword is a work that has to be done through the domestic policy which must be adopted by a national government. To see that the work of forging these arms is assured, and to recruit the men who will bear them, that is the task of the foreign policy.
Reynal-Hitchcock translation: mighty sword. To forge this sword is the task of the domestic political leadership of a people; to guard the work of forging and to seek comrades in arms is the task of the foreign-policy leadership.

MEIN KAMPF

CORRECT

Ford translation: It is the responsibility of the national leaders to forge that sword through their foreign policy. The purpose of this foreign policy must be the securing of weapons and finding allies.

Murphy said the *forging of the sword* was done through *domestic policy* but this contradicts the previous paragraphs which were about foreign policy. The actual German wording said that domestic leadership's job was to forge the sword through a **foreign** policy aimed at gaining weapons and allies, as shown in the correct Ford translation.

Both Murphy and RH missed the original reference saying "weapons and allies" where they only listed allies.
Reynal mistakenly translated it as "work of forging and to seek comrades" The original German word was comrades but this was confusing due to previous usage of the word comrades and it actually meant allies so the Ford translation used allies which makes Hitler's true meaning clearer.

Murphy says "recruit those who will bear them", but this is part of his misunderstanding with the word "domestic". He thought the passage referred to recruiting soldiers internally, when it actually referred to gaining allies(his confusion over the word comrades).

INACCURATE

Reynal-Hitchcock translation: ...not only would it have interrupted or even terminated the internationalizing of German economy and labor power: the internal political effects consequent on a fight for liberation in foreign policy would also be fatal in the future to the present holders of powers of the Reich.

CORRECT

Ford translation: Not only would it have interrupted or even ended the process of making the German economy and workers dependent on other nations, which was the internationalization of Germany, but beyond that, the political effect within Germany resulting from a battle to make Germany free from dependence on foreign countries would have had disastrous consequences later on for the present representatives of the Reich's government.

MEIN KAMPF

The RH-translation says "fight for the liberation in foreign policy". This was incorrect and skewed the meaning of the entire paragraph. This RH translation actually contradicts previous statements. The idea being described was that if Germany were able to form alliances and establish herself as a sovereign nation, and Germany was less dependent on other nations economically, it would be a stronger country and the leaders would then face problems maintaining their positions in the government. The Ford translation is correct and easier to understand. Reynal misunderstood the meaning of this sentence and translated it to mean "liberation in foreign policy'"which does not express the original meaning.

INACCURATE

Murphy translation: But what was feared most of all was that a successful effort to make the REICH independent of foreign countries might have an influence in domestic politics which one day would turn out disastrous for those who now hold supreme power in the government of the REICH. One cannot imagine the revival of a nation unless that revival be preceded by a process of nationalization. Conversely, every important success in the field of foreign politics must call forth a favourable reaction at home.

Reynal-Hitchcock translation: Not only would such a development contradict the inner meaning of the November crime, not only would it have interrupted or even terminated the internationalizing of German economy and labor power: the internal political effects consequent on a fight for liberation in foreign policy would also be fatal in the future to the present holders of powers of the Reich. One can simply not conceive of a nation's rebellion without its previous nationalization, as, conversely, every mighty success in foreign policy necessarily has similar repercussions.

CORRECT

Ford translation: What they feared the most was any effort that would make the Reich independent of foreign countries. Such an effort could eventually be disastrous to those in power who want to make the country dependent on international elements. A revolution within a nation can never occur unless it is preceded by a period where strong national sentiment is built and the people's patriotic spirit

MEIN KAMPF

is nationalized to a fevered pitch. Conversely, huge foreign policy successes have repercussions among the people which can also create patriotic feelings and therefore have the same result.

> The last lines of the older translations are supposed to contradict the previous statement, and even say *Conversely*, however they do not contradict it. Instead they make an unrelated statement which makes no sense within the context of the passage. The Ford translation is the correct interpretation.

INACCURATE

Reynal-Hitchcock translation: One can simply not conceive of a nation's rebellion without its previous nationalization, as, conversely, every mighty success in foreign policy necessarily has similar repercussions.

CORRECT

Ford translation: What they feared the most was any effort that would make the Reich independent of foreign countries. Such an effort could eventually be disastrous to those in power who want to make the country dependent on international elements. A revolution within a nation can never occur unless it is preceded by a period where strong national sentiment is built and the people's patriotic spirit is nationalized to a fevered pitch. Conversely, huge foreign policy successes have repercussions among the people which can also create patriotic feelings and therefore have the same result.

> The RH-translation shows a common translation problem when translating from German. The end of a German sentence refers back to elements earlier in the sentence or to understood elements(like saying "Go to the store" where "you" is understood). The translator did not understand what is being said so he translated the words literally. This pattern is seen in all of the older translations. The result comes out as gibberish. This pattern of literally translating the end of a sentence by Reynal repeats itself many times throughout their version. The Ford translation correctly translated the passage.

MEIN KAMPF

Original German: ...Frankreich arbeitet es mit dem erkann- ten und richtig eingeschätzten Chauvinismus, in England mit wirtschaftlichen und ...

INACCURATE

>**Stackpole translation:** In France it is with the recognized and correctly evaluated chauvinism, in England with economic...

>**Reynal-Hitchcock translation:** France it employs the well-known and well-understood chauvinism;

>**Murphy translation:** In France they exploit the well-known and accurately estimated chauvinistic spirit.

>**Manheim translation:** ...in France they work with the well-known and correctly estimated chauvinism;...

CORRECT

>**Ford translation:** In France, its weapon is easily recognized and they have evaluated its power correctly, it is the fanatical patriotism of the French.

>>None of the older texts define chauvinism but they all use the same word. Today it has a clear meaning of being prejudiced which is not the meaning it had in the original German. The meaning here is a militant devotion to one's country, or a fanatical patriotism of the French in this case.

>>The German word was *Chauvinismus* which all of the older translators used directly, without regard to how English speakers would interpret the passage. Only the Ford translation replaces the German word Chauvinismus with a corrected phrase that makes the actual meaning of the sentence clear. The average person today would have no idea what the passage truly meant if it used the word chauvinism.

MEIN KAMPF

Original German: Allein gerade in die-ser Identität liegt eine immense Gefahr für Deutsch-land.

INACCURATE

Manheim translation: But in this very identity there lies an immense danger for Germany.
Reynal-Hitchcock translation: In this very identity lies an immense danger for Germany.
Murphy translation: This identity of views constitutes an immense, danger for Germany.
Stackpole translation: This very identity constitutes an immense danger for Germany.

CORRECT

Ford translation: The fact that both views are along the same lines constitutes a huge danger for Germany.

> The old translations use the word *identity* which is misleading.. Identity implies an identification, but in this sentence it actually meant an identical quality, as in two aspects of France were identical which created a danger to Germany. It had nothing to actually do with the identity of France. The definition of identity has an alternate meaning "the quality of being the same as something else" which is almost unheard of in English speaking/writing where we would say identical instead, but the alternate meaning is used here.
>
> The confusion is over the German word Identität which if you look it up in a German-English dictionary it does mean identity in English. However it is not the best definition in this translation. This difference is only recognized by actually reading and understanding the paragraph, not just the sentence or just the word, and certainly not by a mechanical word substitution.

MEIN KAMPF

Original German: Und das deutsche Bürgertum führt um die deutsche Zukunft keinen politischen Kampf, weil es diese Zukunft in der aufbauenden Arbeit der Wirtschaft genügend gesichert vermeint.

INACCURATE

Murphy translation: And the people of Germany did not wage any political fight for the future of their country because they thought that the future could be sufficiently secured by constructive work in the economic field.

CORRECT

Ford translation: The German privileged-class will not fight for the future of Germany in a political battle because it believes the future is secured adequately through building up the economy.

> Murphy omitted *bourgeoisie* or privileged-class here. That was an important part of the sentence. As Murphy has translated the passage, it appears he is saying *the masses did not wage a political fight,* but this is incorrect, the meaning was that *the upper ruling classes did not wage a political fight.* The meaning is completely lost by omitting one critical word.

INACCURATE

Stackpole translation: The Revolution of November 1918 was not brought about by trade-unions, but it prevailed over them.
Manheim translation: The revolution of November, 1918, was not made by the trade unions, but was accomplished against them.

CORRECT

Ford translation: The Revolution of November, 1918 was not caused by trade-unions, but it prevailed in spite of them.

> The Stackpole Translation mistranslated this sentence to say *the revolution prevailed over the trade-unions* which is not the meaning of the original German. The original, as shown in the Ford translation meant the Revolution *was successful in spite of trade unions.* This is a completely different meaning, the difference between **dominance over** and **ineffectiveness**. Stackpole is filled with such mistakes.

MEIN KAMPF

The Manheim translation says the revolution was brought *against them* but that is simply not true and contradicts the rest of the paragraph. The phrase "in spite of them" is the correct translation.

INACCURATE

Murphy translation: such a person would be fit to rank with the very greatest men our nation has produced and his bust should be installed in the Valhalla at Regensburg for the admiration of posterity.

CORRECT

Ford translation: A carved bust of him would have needed to find a place in the Valhalla at Regensburg for the sake of posterity. (*Regensburg is a Bavarian city where the Walhalla Temple is located which is a hall-of-fame type building in classic Roman style built in 1807 to commemorate great figures in ethnic German history. It includes a marble interior with busts of famous people.*)

The Ford translation has added explanations for people and places or any unclear concepts. The old translations did not include any explanations for these. RH had some footnotes, but they were very limited. Without knowing what they mean, and some are rather obscure to the modern reader, the meaning of the passage is completely lost and you miss much of the heroic sentiment Hitler used.

Original German: Statt im politischen Kampf zu ringen für die gewonnene Einsicht und Überzeugung, gehen sie dann nur mehr in ihren „Sied-lungs"-Gedanken auf und sitzen am Ende meistens zwischen allen Stühlen.

INACCURATE

Reynal-Hitchcock translation: Instead of struggling in a political fight for the knowledge and the conviction they have won, they more and more wrap themselves in their 'settlement' ideas, and in the end, in most cases, they find themselves between two stools.
Manheim translation: page 604 Instead of fighting in the political struggle for the insight and conviction they have won, they give themselves up entirely to the idea of 'settlement,' and in the end as a rule find themselves holding the bag.
Murphy translation: Instead of participating in the political conflict

MEIN KAMPF

on behalf of the opinions and convictions which they have been brought to accept they will now go further with their 'settlement' idea and in the end they will find themselves for the most part sitting on the ground amidst all the stools.

CORRECT

Ford translation: Instead of fighting in a political battle for the insight and convictions they have gained, they become totally absorbed in their dream of a cottage settlement. In the end, they find themselves sitting between the chairs. (A reference to a German saying "Trying to sit on all of the chairs and ending up sitting between them" which actually means torn between conflicting interests, however here it more specifically means torn between two interests and ending up with nothing, or not sitting on a chair at all.).

> Manheim does not understand the reference so he makes up a new one "holding the bag" and he also uses the literal translation for "settlement". Though it has an equivalent English meaning, we do not normally use the word in this manner. It means house or cottage but we would use it to describe a housing development, as in a settling down. Manheim did not understand the meaning so he translated it literally. Holding the bag is also the wrong saying. The original was a proverb which is a pithy saying in common use that expresses a truth. Holding the bag is an idiom which is an expression that has no meaning in its elements but has meaning within the language. So Manheim inappropriately swapped out a proverb for an idiom, which is simply not acceptable in a translation because it changes the meaning. Furthermore, the holding-the-bag reference is completely wrong because it misstates the meaning of the sentence. It implies the person is left with the blame when in fact the original German meant the person is left without a chair to sit on.

> Hitler used a saying which was unfamiliar to Murphy and Reynal. They thought it literally meant "between all chairs". Only the Ford translation correctly translated it as "no chair at all" meaning the person will lose focus on the fight when his interests are split and lose everything as a result. Missing such important details makes *Mein Kampf* appear confusing when it is actually translation errors that are confusing. The Ford translation both preserved the original saying and included an explanation to make the meaning clear thereby preserving the style and making it understandable.

> The original German saying "zwischen zwei/den/allen Stühlen sitzen" references a conflict of interest. It doesn't mean that the

MEIN KAMPF

chair is pulled out from under you. It means that you're torn between two (or more) opposing opinions or parties. However, in this particular usage, it actually means, torn between two interests and ending up with nothing even if that part is only implied. Understanding a passage like this requires a deeper understanding of what is being said which goes beyond the words on the page.

Later in *Mein Kampf* this reference is repeated:

Original German-second usage: Das Ergebnis die-ses Versuches, sich auf alle Stühle setzen zu wollen, war der bekannte Fall zwischen dieselben, und der Weltkrieg bildete nur die letzte dem Reiche vorgelegte Quittung über seine verfehlte Leitung nach außen.

CORRECT

Ford translation: What made this even worse was the leadership's way of thinking; they believed these policies would help them avoid any armed conflict. They tried to sit on all the chairs at the same time and the result was the proverbial fall between the chairs.

Interestingly, Hitler referenced this same proverb twice in Volume 2 of *Mein Kampf*.
Both instances read "Stühle", i.e. "chairs". "Stools" would be "Hocker" or "Schemel". "Stuhl" can only be translated as "stool" if the medical term is meant. Therefore Murphy's stool translation is inaccurate, though understandable.

Original German: Schon aus diesem Grunde konnte also in der Vorkriegs- zeit die waffenmäßige Vorbereitung für eine Erwerbung von Grund und Boden in Europa nur eine mäßige sein, so
daß der Unterstützung durch zweckmäßige Bundesgenossen nur schwer zu entraten war.

INACCURATE

Murphy translation: That is why, in pre-War times, the military preparation necessary to enable us to conquer new territory in Europe was only very mediocre, so that it was difficult to obtain the support of really helpful allies.

Reynal-Hitchcock translation: For this reason alone, then, the armed preparation of the pre-War period for a conquest of soil and territory in Europe
could be only of such magnitude that support by suitable allies could

MEIN KAMPF

hardly be dispensed with.

CORRECT

> **Ford translation:** Because of this failure, preparing arms in order to acquire new land in Europe could only be done in moderation during the prewar days; that is why we could not advise against accepting the help of proper allies.
>
>> Here Murphy translates the passage as "difficult to obtain the support of the allies", but this is incorrect. As shown in the corrected Ford translation and in the RH-translation, the passage actually said "support from allies is difficult to dispense with" meaning Germany needed strong allies, it did not mean it was difficult to obtain allies.
>>
>> The RH translation, "difficult to dispense with" is a somewhat liberal translation as well. The most accurate translation for "entraten" is "disadvise", rendering this passage something like "such that support by appropriate allies was hardly disadvised/ill-advised." The Ford translation make the best use of the sentence and keeps it in a structure that is understandable and accurate.

Original German:...das sonst mögliche Bündnis mit England, ohne aber nun logischerweise sich auf Rußland zu stützen, und stolperte endlich, von allen, außer dem habsburgischen Erbübel, ver-lassen, in den Weltkrieg hinein.

INACCURATE

> **Murphy translation:** Finally they stumbled into the World War, abandoned by all except the ill-starred Habsburgs.
> **Reynal-Hitchcock translation:**...and finally the government stumbled into the World War, abandoned by all except for the Habsburg hereditary evil.

CORRECT

> **Ford translation:** Deserted by all would-be allies except the Hapsburg shiesters, we finally stumbled into the First World War.

Murphy mistranslated the passage as *ill-starred*. The RH-translation was overly literal when they translated as *hereditary evil*.

The meaning of *Erbübel* is *hereditary evil* which is the correct **literal** translation, however that was not the **meaning**. There's a good chance that *übel* has a slightly different meaning in this case. Not evil like the Devil but having been given a raw deal. The German-English dictionary translates Erbübel as *deep-rooted failing* or *ingrained failing*. Since the discussion is about the monarchy, it appears to mean "*those guys who have given us a raw deal through generations*" or even more accurately considering the context as "*those shiesters we had to make a deal with*". Or we could say someone who will not deal fairly or cannot deal fairly. This is another example of the difficulties in translating from one language to another. Translations are not always clear-cut.

The spelling difference of Habsburg and Hapsburg is not an error. These are simply alternate spellings, however the Hapsburg is more common in English.

Original German: Daß sich dabei England aller Staaten als Bundesgenossen bediente, die militärisch über-haupt in Frage kommen konnten, entsprach ebensosehr seiner traditionellen Vorsicht in der Abschätzung der Kraft des Gegners als der Einsicht in die augenblickliche eigene Schwäche.

INACCURATE

> **Murphy translation:** In carrying out this policy, England allied herself with those countries which had a definite military importance. And that was in keeping with her traditional caution in estimating the power of her adversary and also in recognizing her own temporary weakness.

CORRECT

> **Ford translation:** England's effort to secure as allies all the states that could eventually provide military assistance was the natural result of her traditional caution in estimating the strength of her opponent and her own weakness at the time.
>
>> Murphy translates the passage as "temporary weakness" but the original German meant "at the time" or literally augenblickliche translates to present/immediate or "current" not temporary.

Original German: Mit der Revolutionierung Deutschlands fand die britische Sorge einer drohenden germanischen Welthegemonie ihre für die englische Staatskunst erlösende Beendigung.

MEIN KAMPF

INACCURATE

Stackpole translation: When Germany turned revolutionary, the British worries with respect to a threatening German world hegemony ceased in a way quite satisfactory to British statesmanship.
Reynal-Hitchcock translation: With the inner revolutionizing of Germany, the British concern with a threatening German world hegemony met an end which liberated British statecraft.
Murphy translation: When the German Revolution took place England's fears of a German world hegemony came to a satisfactory end.

CORRECT

Ford translation: With the Revolution in Germany, the British worries about a threatening German world domination ended in redemption, the British felt their fears had been justified.

> Reynal says "end which liberated British statecraft" and Murphy says "came to a satisfactory end". The RH and Murphy both misunderstood the passage. The original German literally translates to "..English statesmanship redemptive ending." meaning their fears ended in redemption or stated another way they were justified. The Ford translation shows the corrected translation. The Stackpole Translation makes sense but it is inaccurate.

INACCURATE

Murphy translation: If such a leader cannot be found it is futile to struggle with Fate and even more foolish to try to overthrow the existing state of things without being able to construct a better in its place.

CORRECT

Ford translation: If such a great man cannot be found, then it is useless to argue with Fate and it is even more foolish to force the issue and charge ahead using men who are poor substitutes for greatness.

> Murphy says "construct a better in its place" but this is not what the original text said. The original said that it was *senseless to attack the enemy with a man who was a poor substitute for a great man* and said nothing about constructing better organizations.

93

MEIN KAMPF

INACCURATE

> **Murphy translation:** Here again, as everywhere else, the inflexible principle must be observed, that the interests of the country must come before party interests.

CORRECT

> **Ford translation:** The iron principle that the Fatherland comes first and then the Party must always apply.
>
> > Murphy dropped the line about the *Fatherland first then party* and he changed it to country.

Original German: Nein, eine Macht, die selbst auf Ansehen hält und die von Bündnissen sich mehr erhofft als Provisionen für beutehungrige Parlamentarier, wird sich mit dem derzeiti-gen Deutschland nicht verbünden, ja, sie kann es nicht.

INACCURATE

> **Murphy translation:** No. A self-respecting Power which expects something more from alliances than commissions for greedy Parliamentarians will not and cannot enter into an alliance with our present-day Germany.
> **Reynal-Hitchcock translation:** No; a power which has respect for itself and which hopes for more from allies than provender for booty-hungry parliamentarians would not ally itself with contemporary Germany, yes, cannot do it.
> **Manheim translation:** No, a power which itself wants to be respected and which hopes to gain more from alliances than fees for hungry parliamentarians will not ally itself with present-day Germany; indeed, it cannot.

CORRECT

> **Ford translation:** No. A power that has any self-respect and expects more from an alliance than to pay commissions to interest-hungry parliamentarians will not enter an alliance with the Germany of today; this is something they simply cannot do.

94

MEIN KAMPF

The last sentence where the RH-translation says "yes, cannot do it" makes no sense. Murphy omits the line completely. Only the Ford translation includes the correct meaning which is "It would be impossible." The literal translation is "yes, they cannot", but in English this makes no sense and appears tacked on. This is another example where the translator must understand what is being translated and not mechanically substitute words. The original German also says "a power that holds itself to prestige" which means *has self-respect*. Manheim mistranslated this as "wants to be respected".

Original German: Wie so oft in der Geschichte, ist in dem gewaltigen Ringen Deutschland der große Drehpunkt. Werden unser Volk und unser Staat das Opfer dieser blutund geldgierigen jüdischen Völkertyrannen, so sinkt die ganze Erde in die Umstrickung dieses Polypen; befreit sich Deutschland aus dieser Umklammerung, so darf diese größte Völkergefahr als für die gesamte Welt gebrochen gelten.

INACCURATE

Murphy translation: As has so often happened in history, Germany is the chief pivot of this formidable struggle. If our people and our State should fall victims to these oppressors of the nations, lusting after blood and money, the whole earth would become the prey of that hydra.

Reynal-Hitchcock translation: Thus, as so often in history, the mighty struggle within Germany is the great turning-point. If our people and our State fall victims to this bloodthirsty and moneythirsty Jewish tyrant over nations, then the whole world will fall into this polyp's net;...

Manheim translation: ... of these bloodthirsty and avaricious Jewish tyrants of nations, the whole earth will sink into the snares of this octopus; ...

CORRECT

Ford translation: As it has happened so often in history, Germany is again in the middle of the huge struggle. If our people and our state become victims of these money-obsessed Jewish bloody tyrants, then the whole world will be ensnared by this octopus.

The RH-translation says "into this polyp's net".
Murphy translates the same passage as "become the prey of that hydra" and Manheim says "snare of this octopus". The original German was "Umstrickung dieses Polypen" which literally translates to ensnared polyps and the true meaning of the passage is "...then the whole Earth sinks into the ensnarement of these

polyps." The German word Umstrickung means ensnarement.

Polyp has a dictionary definition of a creature that is an invertebrate like a jellyfish or coral. It is hollow and has many arms or tentacles. If you look up this definition it has a meaning of hydra, however this is not the mythical hydra, it is a type of coral. A hydra is a type of freshwater polyp of genus Hydra which is a cylindrical body creature with a mouth surrounded by tentacles. That is clearly not what Hitler meant.
Either way you choose to translate this passage, polyp-growth or a sea creature name would be more correct and not the mythical hydra.

The two most common meanings in German are "octopus" and the medical polyp (an abnormal growth and spreading of tissue). It never means the mythical Hydra which would be directly referred to as Hydra in German. The Ford translation went with octopus because it fits with *ensnared* and here wart or growth would not make sense. This was a great example of how translations can vary with the same source passage.

Original German: Wie so oft in der Geschichte, ist in dem gewaltigen Ringen Deutschland der große Drehpunkt.

INACCURATE

>**Manheim translation:** As often in history, Germany is the great pivot in the might struggle.
>**Reynal-Hitchcock translation:** Thus, as so often in history, the mighty struggle within Germany is the great turning-point.
>**Murphy translation:** As has so often happened
in history, Germany is the chief pivot of this formidable struggle.

CORRECT

>**Ford translation:** As it has happened so often in history, Germany is again in the middle of a huge struggle.
>
>The older translations used an overly literal translation of *pivot point*. The RH-translation misunderstood it as turning-point which completely changes the meaning. Germany was not the turning-point in this sentence, they were *in the middle* which is shown in the corrected Ford translation.

MEIN KAMPF

Original German: Der Unfug dieser Vertretungen ist um so größer, als ihnen neben den Schäden nicht der geringste Nutzen zugeschrieben werden kann.

INACCURATE

Reynal-Hitchcock translation: The nuisance of these missions is all the greater since there cannot be ascribed to them the slightest utility to counterbalance their harmfulness.
Murphy translation: The absurdity of these 'representations' is all the greater because they do harm and do not bring the slightest advantage.
Stackpole translation: The folly of maintaining such legations is all the greater, since besides doing harm they are perfectly useless.
Manheim: The mischief of these missions is all the greater as not the least benefit can be attributed to them along with the harm.

CORRECT

Ford translation: The foolishness of maintaining such delegations is even greater because they do more harm than good.

> Here, Hitler actually used a common saying, which also exists in English, "*more harm than good*". None of the older translations recognized this common saying which is why it is only in the Ford translation.

INACCURATE

Murphy translation: The follower is one whom the propaganda has converted to the doctrine of the movement.
Reynal-Hitchcock translation: The follower is inclined to like a movement by its propaganda.

CORRECT

Ford translation: A follower is won over to the movement by propaganda.

> The RH-translation implies the follower "likes" a movement. This is not accurate. The actual German meant "the follower is converted to the beliefs of the movement" not that he simply likes it. The Ford translation is more accurate and easier to understand. Murphy is in between.

MEIN KAMPF

INACCURATE

Reynal-Hitchcock translation: As already stressed, the germ cells for the estate chambers will have to rest in the various vocational representations, that means above all in the trade unions.
Murphy translation: As I have already said, the germ cells of this State must lie in the administrative chambers which will represent the various occupations and professions, therefore first of all in the trades unions.

CORRECT

Ford translation: As I have emphasized, the germ-cells for the council of economics will come from the various bodies that represent the trade-unions.

> The RH-translation translated the passage with "estate chambers" which should refer to economic commissions that will be created by the new National Socialist State. Reynal translated the words without understanding what they meant and picked a common meaning, but not the correct meaning.
>
> Murphy was closer but either did not recognize or left out the fact that the administration was an economic administration in the form of chambers or structures, like a chamber of judges, where chamber means a board or council of high ranking officials. It was changed to council in Ford translation because chamber is not used in this way in English except in certain rare circumstances like a chamber of judges. The average person might misunderstand chamber to mean a room or division so the Ford translation went with the clearest English wording.

INACCURATE

Murphy translation: In contradistinction to the enormous number of papers in Jewish hands, there was at that time only one important newspaper that defended the cause of the people. This was a matter for grave consideration. As I have often learned by experience, the reason for that state of things must be attributed to the incompetent way in which the business side of the so-called popular newspapers was managed.
Reynal-Hitchcock translation: Looked at objectively, the fact that

MEIN KAMPF

in the face of the enormous Jewish press there existed not a single really important folkish newspaper was bound to cause reflection. As afterwards I was able to determine in praxis innumerable times, this was due for the greater part to the unbusinesslike management of so-called folkish enterprises on the whole.

CORRECT

Ford translation: It gives a person food for thought if you notice that, in contrast to the enormous number of Jewish newspapers, there is only one important racial-Nationalist newspaper. Later, I had the chance to learn first hand why this was so. Most of the so-called populist enterprises were not managed in a business-like manner.

> Murphy translated the passage with "popular newspapers", but it should have been populist newspaper. Even that translation does not indicate the true meaning. The passage means racial newspapers. He also says "the cause of the people" at the start which was actually supposed to be another race reference and not a general reference to all people.
> An important part of the meaning was lost in this mistranslation. This is corrected in the Ford translation. Both race and populist are in the same passage and both have similar meanings, however populist means people-concerned-with-race in *Mein Kampf*. We see the same situation for the RH-translation which said folkish instead of race.

INACCURATE

Murphy translation: These were conducted too much according to the rule that opinion should prevail over action that produces results. Quite a wrong standpoint, for opinion is of itself something internal and finds its best expression in productive activity.

CORRECT

Ford translation: They followed the idea that loyalty is more essential than success. This point of view is entirely false. Loyalty in itself is not something that can be seen. It is best expressed through accomplishment.

> Murphy translated the words but again missed the *meaning*. The "action that produces results" was clearly "success" which is easier to understand and more correct based on Hitler's previous chapters and fits the topic of success which was being discussed. This is a

MEIN KAMPF

good example which shows that neither the RH-translation style of direct translation nor the Murphy style of re-stating worked to accurately represent the original *Mein Kampf* text.

INACCURATE

Murphy translation: The VÖLKISCHE BEOBACHTER was a so-called 'popular' organ, as its name indicated. It had all the good qualities, but still more the errors and weaknesses, inherent in all popular institutions.

Reynal-Hitchcock translation: The Voelkischer Beobachter also as its name already indicates was a so-called 'folkish' organ with all the advantages and even more the faults and the weaknesses which are characteristic of folkish institutions.

CORRECT

Ford translation: As the name indicates, the Race Watcher newspaper was called a "racial-Nationalist" mouthpiece and it had all the strengths connected with such institutions, but it also had all the faults and weaknesses.

Both old translations use the word *organ* which is technically correct, however it does not make the meaning of the passage clear. Organ has a secondary dictionary meaning of newspaper or voice or channel or mouthpiece. The meaning here was very specific and the use of organ to say *a means of disbursing information* is uncommon in English. The first impulse is to assume it means the paper was an "arm" of the party, but that is not the true meaning which is why it was changed in the Ford translation to reflect its true meaning more and not the literal, mechanical translation as in the old translations. Also, the German name had already been established, so in this follow-up passage the English name was used which is easier to read and clearer. It was also unnecessary to give a German name and then to tell an English reader "as the name indicates" when the English reader cannot tell what the name indicates. Even the translators were confused about what it meant.

The translation of folkish and "popular institutions" by Murphy were actually referring to race-based institutions. If the reader did not know this was the real meaning he would not fully understand what the passage was about.

Murphy dropped the R to get VÖLKISCHE and RH changed it to Voelkischer with no pronunciation marks and changed the spelling. These may have been typographical errors or translation errors.

100

MEIN KAMPF

Völkischer Beobachter

The newspaper Völkischer Beobachter was acquired by the NSDAP. It was an existing newspaper they purchased. There has been much controversy over the translation of the name. Most past translators used a simplistic and literal translation which yielded Folkish Observer, Ethnic Observer or People's Observer. Though these are technically accurate, none represent the content of the paper. The literal translation is Ethnic Observers which still lacks the meaning of the original. This is an excellent example of how many translation efforts face hard choices. The translator focuses on the words and tries to determine a one-for-one substitution for a word in the target language. The result is a title like Folkish Observer which has no meaning to English speakers.

The first part, Völkischer, means ethnic or race and the way Hitler's used it he means specifically and exclusively the Germanic race. The second part, Beobachter, means observer in the most literal sense, however, the word origin is more interesting and it has a more specific meaning here which is not the *observer* meaning you will find in a German-English dictionary.

Common sense tells you that the titles Folkish Observer, Ethnic Observer or People's Observer are weak translations because English speakers simply do not talk like that. Hitler would never have used such a name either because it does not deliver the message he wanted to deliver. Those titles are passive, impotent, and make no strong statement, which is completely contrary to his theories on propaganda. They also do not provide any visual imagery which Hitler was well known to generate in his speeches.

In the 2009 Ford Translation of *Mein Kampf*, the newspaper name was translated as **Race Watcher** which was more true to the original paper name. This would attract more attention than the sterile Ethnic Observer which makes Race Watcher a more accurate interpretation of the title and is within the style of Hitler's propaganda. The paper name is frequently translated as People's Observer. This may be a valid direct translation for someone using a German-English dictionary and going no further in his research, but it ignores the subtext and meaning of the title.

If the Ku Klux Klan published an English paper called "*Our People*" and this were directly translated into another language using their word for *people*, meaning all people, it would be a gross misrepresentation of the meaning of the title. The same is true in the case when translating Völkischer Beobachter to English. To translate it as *People's Observer* is to ignore the content and the deeper meaning of the title's words in German, not to mention ignoring the context and common understanding of the terms in the 1930's.

MEIN KAMPF

Based on the most common usage of these words:
>Völkisch:
>The best translation would be "nationalistic / national", second best "racial"

>Beobachter:
>Best translation would be "Watcher", second best "Look-out" (as in a sentry or guard), NOT Observer!

Völkischer Beobachter translated as National Watcher represents the most common use of the words. This does not make it the correct translation in this instance.

"Beobachter" is certainly derived from "Watchtower" in some way, but the Germans of the 1930's would not have been aware of that. The verb "beobachten" is simply too common for too many different tasks and not used to describe a military/guarding situation.

Translating it as Racialist-Watcher could be even more correct than the previous attempts. However, this was not originally used in the Ford translation because in English we would not say "Racialist Watcher" and the purpose of the Ford translation was to make *Mein Kampf* easier to understand for English speakers while maintaining the highest possible accuracy.

Race Watchers is a better representation in English because it implies actively watching, not passively observing. If that does not make sense, think of it as "*I am watching and guarding, I am actively protecting*" versus "*I am observing you from a distance*". One is clearly passive and the other is clearly active, almost threatening. Because of this difference, the Ford translation uses Race Watcher. It is a better English representation, it implies active motives and Race (specifically the Germanic race) is, of course, the intent of the original title, not people, populist, folkish, or ethnic. Those are general terms as well which are weak. If Hitler were to publish an English language version of his paper, he surely would have called it Race Watcher because the other names are weak and have no visual strength.

The older translators either never translated the name and used the German wording or they used the name People's Observer, Folkish Observer, Ethnic Observer, or Populist Observer, all of which are misleading and not the intent of the name. Hitler did not want a newspaper that had an obtuse title. He wanted people to know what was in it and to be motivated to pick it up.

Author Larry Camp made a persuasive argument for the name Germanic Watchtower. This translation may at first seem like a great leap from the original wording, but if we do some research, it can be justified and shown to be a possible interpretation. It was not used because it feels like too much of a stretch in the meaning. The average German in the 1930's would not have interpreted Watchtower from Beobachter even if the root and entomology suggests it. Such an image also keeps within Hitler's style and is something that would have appealed to his personality. He may have seen this in the title where

MEIN KAMPF

others did not.

This imagery is paralleled in the song Watcher On The Rhine which Hitler knew well and mentioned in *Mein Kampf*. The imagery of a Watcher/Watchtower in relation to military matters is also common in German writing of the time(and earlier). The militaristic history of Germany has many images of a strong silent sentry soldier on guard, watching, protecting, which made the Germans feel secure and strong. A similar example can be drawn from English in the word cadence. This word is usually associated with military marching, however, the definition is balanced, rhythmic flow, as in poetry or speaking. In English, when we hear the word *cadence*, we generally think of a marching military parade and not of poetry. Similarly, Beobachter, has a historically military association in the German language, though subtle.

Germanic or Teutonic Watchtower is an interesting translation but is not used in the Ford translation because it is too far from what the average German would have read into the name.

"Watcher" is a valid choice and the German title clearly meant something "active". Another possible translation would be "look-out" as in a sentry or guard. This option was not used because Watcher was more appropriate.

Racial or Race were used. Germanic and Teutonic are both strong options because the race Hitler was talking about was the German race. The title could be interpreted as Germanic Watcher, but if Hitler had wanted that title he would have used Germanic and not a People/Race word.

Ultimately, the best translation for Völkischer Beobachter which is true to the original words, includes the imagery that would have appealed to Hitler, and best represents the subject-matter of the paper in the English language is **Race Watcher.** This is the translation used in the Ford translation of *Mein Kampf* as well.

To further justify the Race Watcher translation, I have included a research map(Appendix B) which shows the common uses of the terms from various sources. Although this map is not comprehensive and it was not used during the translation of *Mein Kampf* and none of the translations in the book were based on any consensus of translation choices and a higher level of skill was needed, plus the map was generated after the Ford translation went to press, this map does justify the translation choices in a statistical way. It shows National/Nationalistic as the first choice for Völkischer and Racial as the second. Then it shows Watcher as the first choice for Beobachter, Look-Out is second, Watchtower is third, and Observer is the fourth choice. This again confirms the Race Watcher translation is a valid translation.

After the translation was questioned by a number of people, I was glad to go back and review the research and reasoning behind the original translation and I am pleased that the original Race Watcher choice has turned out to be the correct choice. The translation of Hitler's newspaper name is very important and is something that should be represented in English properly.

We are not finished yet. Let's take a closer look at the individual words. "Beobachter", according to the Deutsches Wörterbuch (DWB, "German Dictionary") started by the Grimm brothers in 1838, is defined as a faithful watcher of nature, a sharp and precise observer. ["BEOBACHTER, m. observator: ein treuer beobachter der natur; ein scharfer, feiner beobachter., Deutsches Wörterbuch von Jacob Grimm und Wilhelm Grimm. Band 1, Spalten 1478 - 1480)]. The "Sprach-Brockhaus", a dictionary of 1951, states that Beobachter is someone who watches/traces events exactly/accurately. ["Wer Vorgänge genau verfolgt", Der Sprach-Brockhaus, Wiesbaden, Brockhaus, 1951. p. 72]. **Note that neither of these uses the word** *Observer*.

Adolf Hitler wrote about the "Völkischer Beobachter that its purpose should be - besides supporting the fight of the national-socialists - to help form a consistent direction of the movement, which suggests that for the Nazis the word "Bebobachter" in the newspapers title carries as well the meaning to "watch" out for heretics of the official party-line [Adolf Hitler: "[die Zeitung solle die Partei] nicht nur in ihrem Kampfe nach außen unterstützen, sondern auch mithelfen, im Inneren der "Bewegung" jene einheitliche Richtung tonangebend zu bestimmen, ohne die eine innere Einheit der Partei nicht denkbar wäre". Völkischer Beobachter, 26.2.1925, Seite 2)]. Therefor a translation of "Beobachter" as "watcher" in the context of the "Völkischer Beobachter" is well justified.

"Völkisch" etymologically derives apparently from the latin word "popularis"- "belonging to the nation" - often [especially during the Nazi-era] with special emphasis on Volk and race. ["zunächst für lat. popularis - "zum Volk gehörend" [..] dann im Sinne von "National" - häufig [im Nationalsozialismus] mit besonderer Betonung von Volk und Rasse verwendet. Duden Etymologie, Mannheim: Dudenverlag, 1989. p.792).

Walter Jung states in his dissertation concerning the ideology, goals and substance of the German völkisch-movements in the Weimar Republic that this word was used to make the German people appear absolute. Jung concludes as well that the word "völkisch" expresses an inconsiderate and absolutized relationship to their own "Volk", which therefore becomes the highest value - clearly a strong racist/racial connotation ["[...] wurde in und durch die deutschvölkische Ideologie das eigene, deutsche Volk völlig verabsolutiert und zum alleinigen Maßstab, wenn nicht gar zur Inkarnation aller von den Deutschvölkischen als positiv anerkannten Eigenschaften erhoben. [...] daß der Begriff "völkisch" "eine unreflektierte und verabsolutierende Beziehung zum eigenen Volk" ausdrücke, "in der dieses die Stelle eines obersten Wertes" einnehme". Jung, Walter: "Ideologische Voraussetzungen, Inhalte und Ziele außenpolitischer Programmatik und Propaganda in der deutschvölkischen Bewegung der Anfangsjahre der Weimarer Republik – Das Beispiel Deutschvölkischer Schutz- und Trutzbund. Dissertation zur Erlangung des philosophischen Doktorgrades an der Philosophischen Fakultät der Georg August-Universität zu Göttingen" Göttingen, 2000. p.9] The "Völkischer Beobachter" was clearly and heavily racist, especially anti-Semitic. Therefore, and because of the above mentioned emphasis in the 1930s of the word "völkisch on the

MEIN KAMPF

perceived superiority of the German race, a translation of "racial" is appropriate. As previously stated, "Racial Watcher" would not feel right in English so it was simplified to "Race Watcher" which has the same meaning and is more easily digested by the American English ear.

Note: I would like to give special thanks to author and researcher Larry Camp for his assistance in this translation research of Völkischer Beobachter. His insight and research into the word origins has revealed a new aspect to the meaning. Also to Andreas V. for his research in Germany as a native German speaker and researcher.

INACCURATE

Murphy translation: Though its contents were excellent, its management as a business concern was simply impossible.
Reynal-Hitchcock translation: As honorable as its contents were, as impossible, from the business viewpoint, was the management of the enterprise.

CORRECT

Ford translation: The contents of these newspapers were honorable, but the enterprises were managed in a way that made it impossible for them to function as a business.

> Murphy mistranslated noble/honorable as excellent. The RH-translation is also mixed up which makes it very difficult to understand without re-reading several times.

INACCURATE

Murphy translation: The first duty of the propagandist is to win over people who can subsequently be taken into the organization. And the first duty of the organization is to select and train men who will be capable of carrying on the propaganda. The second duty of the organization is to disrupt the existing order of things and thus make room for the penetration of the new teaching which it represents, while the duty of the organizer must be to fight for the purpose of securing power, so that the doctrine may finally triumph.

MEIN KAMPF

CORRECT

Ford translation: The first task of propaganda is to win over men who can be used in the organization; the first task of the organization is to select men who can carry on the propaganda. The second task of propaganda is the destruction of existing conditions so the new doctrine can spread more easily, and the second task of the organization is to fight for power. This power will be needed to secure the final success of the doctrine.

> Murphy translated the passage with the word *organization,* but it should have been **propaganda** as shown in the Ford translation. This is a rather serious error especially considering the emphasis Hitler put on propaganda throughout the book. He also missed part of the translation completely. Previously, the passage said the first duty of propaganda is... and the first duty of the organization is.... and this passage was the follow up and was supposed to say the second duty of propaganda is.... and the second duty of organization is ... however Murphy missed this 2x2 literary structure, missed part of the translation and mistranslated the entire passage as a result.
> This passage was also in chapter 11 of volume 2 which is near the end where his translation became more creative in Murphy's edition.
> Murphy is also confusing in the last part where he says "fight for the purpose of securing power". This statement should have been simply "fight for power".

INACCURATE

Reynal-Hitchcock translation: When propaganda has filled a whole people with an idea, the organization, with the help of a handful of people, can draw the consequences.
Stackpole translation:...a mere handful of men is sufficient to draw the consequences.
Murphy translation: When the propaganda work has converted a whole people to believe in a doctrine, the organization can turn the results of this into practical effect through the work of a mere handful of men.

CORRECT

Ford translation: After propaganda has converted the entire population over to an idea, only a handful of men are needed to finish the job.

MEIN KAMPF

The RH version translates literally by saying "can draw the consequences". This does not make sense. The Ford translation is correct with "..finish the job".

INACCURATE

Reynal-Hitchcock translation: The contrary is frequently the case.
Murphy translation: The contrary is very frequently the case.
Stackpole translation: The contrary is often the case.

CORRECT

Ford translation: The opposite is usually true.

The meaning may be determined from the older translations, but only the Ford translation is truly understandable and in modern English.

INACCURATE

Reynal-Hitchcock translation: Great theorists are only in the rarest cases great organizers, as the greatness of the theorist and the program-maker lies primarily in the recognition and in the establishment of abstractly correct laws, while the organizer has to be primarily a psychologist.
Murphy translation: Great masters of theory are only very rarely great organizers also. And this is because the greatness of the theorist and founder of a system consists in being able to discover and lay down those laws that are right in the abstract, whereas the organizer must first of all be a man of psychological insight.
Stackpole translation: Great theorists are seldom great organizers as the greatness of a theorist lies primarily in the understanding and the establishment of correct, abstract laws, while the organizer must primarily be a psychologist.

CORRECT

Ford translation: Great theorists are rarely great organizers. The greatness of a theorist lies in his ability to understand and establish correct, abstract laws, while the organizer must primarily be an expert in understanding the human mind.

The Stackpole translation and RH-translation said *a leader*

107

MEIN KAMPF

must be a psychologist. Obviously this is not literally true and the meaning can be deduced, but it is a bump in the flow of the material which causes a disconcerting jolt forcing the reader to stop and think. The problem is that the reader is not thinking about the concept being presented. He is trying to figure out what this sentence means. That is not good writing. The Ford translation has the correct meaning clearly spelled out.

INACCURATE

Reynal-Hitchcock translation: The year 1921 had assumed special significance for I me and for the movement in an additional direction.
Murphy translation: The year 1921 was specially important for me from many points of view.
Stackpole translation: THE year 1921 has become important for me and for the movement in more than one respect.

CORRECT

Ford translation: The year 1921 has become important for me and for the movement in many ways.

> The Ford translation uses a common phrase "in many ways" which was the meaning and even the literal translation of the original German, however other translations translated the words and not the meaning. The statements in the older translations of "additional direction' and "many points of view" do not represent Hitler's original words or intent which is clear from the words he used. Reynal interpreted "ways" in German to mean direction which it does not mean here. Murphy understood the meaning, but he missed the correct phrasing.

INACCURATE

Murphy translation: In both cases one attitude determines the other.
Reynal-Hitchcock translation: In both cases the one conditions the other:

CORRECT

Ford translation: In both cases, we can see cause and effect.

> The meaning is shown only in the Ford translation which is a common saying in German and English of "cause and effect". The

MEIN KAMPF

RH-translation and Murphy's translation missed a common saying and translated it literally.

INACCURATE

Reynal-Hitchcock translation: ...representation of German interests abroad must be balanced domestically by a heavier pressure downwards, which, on its part, again requires...

CORRECT

Ford translation: Even here we see that one nail drives another deeper still. Every new obligation that the Reich assumes, as a result of its criminal mis-handling of foreign German interests, creates a stronger blow which falls on the states.

> The RH-translation is unclear where they translated the passage as "pressure downwards". Only when you look at the Ford translation do you truly understand the meaning. The pressure downward meant a striking blow as if from a hammer. It did not mean pressure in the general and indefinite way it was stated by the Reynal translation.

INACCURATE

Reynal-Hitchcock translation: When Kurt Eisner gave the revolutionary uprising in Bavaria a thoroughly conscious impulse against the rest of the Reich, he did not in the slightest degree act on...

CORRECT

Ford translation: When Kurt Eisner intentionally gave the revolutionary uprising in Bavaria the appearance of a spear point aimed at Prussia, he did not do this from the standpoint of Bavarian interests, but only as a commissioner of Jewry.

> The previous paragraph had established that Eisner's actions were intended to turn Bavaria *against* Prussia, not against all of Southern Germany so the Reynal translation is incorrect. The Ford translation is correct. The original German did not

109

say Prussia explicitly but used a phrase which meant the *Large Part of Germany*, and that phrase means Prussia. Such errors are common in older translations where the translators translated sections as if they were in isolation. They ignored the context and translated without noticing contradictory passages in the previous paragraphs. Such instances have made readers think that Hitler contradicted himself in places (which he did at times), however some of these instances are actually the result of poor translations.

INACCURATE

Reynal-Hitchcock translation: Of course, however, this Oriental, who had perpetually run around here and there throughout the rest of Germany

Murphy translation: This Oriental was just about the last person in the world that could be pointed to as the logical defender of Bavarian interests.

Stackpole translation: It was obvious however that precisely this oriental who had constantly wandered about here and there in the rest of Germany as a journalist...

CORRECT

Ford translation: It was obvious that this "valuable gem," who had constantly wandered around Germany as one of the journalist rabble, would be the last person called upon as a protector of Bavarian interests and he was completely indifferent whether Bavaria was even part of God's wide world.

> The original term used was oriental (lower case) however this does not always mean someone from Asia or the Orient, it also means a valuable gemstone and is another way of saying, "He is a gem." Only the Ford version correctly translated this passage.
>
> All other translators gave the impression that this Kurt Eisner, born in Berlin of German Jewish parents was somehow Oriental. This is not the original intent of the passage. It was a sarcastic remark with multiple meanings.
> 1. Using oriental implied Eisner was an alien in the country (since he was Jewish),
> 2. It was sarcastic saying he was a "gem" or valuable when Hitler's real meaning was that he was worthless,
> 3. He was called an oriental, or in longer form an oriental gem, meaning he was the head of the Socialist movement, and two sentences previously, he declared himself the defender of

MEIN KAMPF

Bavarian interests.

Only one translation was correct here and that was the Ford translation. In German the word is orientalisch.

INACCURATE

Stackpole translation: At the same time when a so-called volunteer defense unit in difficulty and despair trains or seeks to train in the idea of defense a few thousand well-meaning men (those of a different sort it does not even approach) -the State itself consistently robs millions of young people of ...
Reynal-Hitchcock translation: ...good-natured in themselves (it cannot get at others at all), the State itself, by the pacifist democratic manner of education, methodically
Murphy translation: ...lack of necessities, try to educate and train a few thousand men of goodwill (the others need not be taken into account) for purposes of national defense...

CORRECT

Ford translation: ...facing difficulty and despair, tries to train a few thousand well-meaning men (those who are not so harmonious simply remain untrained) in the idea of defense, the State itself consistently...

> The passage meant that the militant defense groups trained those who were willing to be trained and had a good temperament and they simply did not bother training those who lacked discipline. This meaning is not clear from any of the older translations. Murphy mistranslated the part in parentheses and the RH-translation also incorrectly translated the passage. The Stackpole Translation is correct but is difficult to understand. Only after you read the Ford translation is the meaning clear.

INACCURATE

Murphy translation: At the station the railway employees informed us all of a sudden that our train would not move.

Stackpole translation: Suddenly we were told at the station that the train would not be run.

111

MEIN KAMPF

CORRECT

Ford translation: When we arrived at the train station, we were suddenly told that the workers refused to run the train for us.

Murphy misunderstood and thought they claimed the train was not functioning, but the original German text indicated the crew refused to run the train. Stackpole stated it in an odd way but translated it as the original, though in a confusing way.

Original German: Damit ziehen wir Nationalsozialisten bewußt einen Strich unter die außenpoli-tische Richtung unserer Vorkriegszeit.

INACCURATE

Manheim translation: And so we National Socialists consciously draw a line beneath the foreign-policy tendency of our pre-War period.

CORRECT

Ford translation: So, we National-Socialists must scratch out the foreign policy practices of the pre-war period.

This passage can be interpreted in two ways. Either Hitler was referring to the pre-Ware period just before World War I which he considered terrible leadership that led to the loss of the war, or he was referring to pre-War times of the more distant past when Germany was strong which he did endorse. The surrounding text makes it appear that he was talking about poor leadership. This also fits with the attack style he used where he spent more time attacking enemies than praising things he liked. This is why the Ford translation went with the interpretation that he was talking about the immediate pre-War period. This analysis is also based on this interpretation.
The Manheim translation says that the Nazi party is to draw a line UNDER, or underline the pre-War policy, thereby highlighting it but this is not what Hitler meant. He was not highlighting the policy and was not signifying its importance, he was slamming previous policy and saying it was to be crossed out, scratched out, a line drawn THROUGH it, not under it. The German language can be interpreted either way, though it does say "Under" this is clearly not Hitler's meaning. It could also be an error in the original German that was not corrected to say strike out or mark

MEIN KAMPF

out. The Ford translation translates both the line and the meaning. The literal translation of *unter* is among and a second most common translation is under, but among or "in the midst of" is the more accurate translation and in English we use a common phrase "draw a line through" which has the same meaning. In this case under means very literally under, not below the word but under the letters or on top of the letters with a line through the center, not below the letters. The passage meant pre-War foreign policy was to be marked out and thrown away to make way for the new foreign policy as shown in the Ford translation which uses scratch out because that was the intent and true meaning of the passage.

INACCURATE

Reynal-Hitchcock translation:...we intended to take with us a few dozens of the brethren of the international solidarity on the locomotive and on the tender, and in each coach.
Murphy translation: that we would drive the train ourselves, but that we would take away with us, in the locomotive and tender and in some of the carriages, a few dozen members of this brotherhood of international solidarity.
Stackpole translation: ...we would operate the train ourselves, planning to take along in the locomotive tender and each coach a few dozen brothers of the international solidarity.

CORRECT

Ford translation: I would also take along a few dozen brothers of the international solidarity in the locomotive, the supply car, and in each passenger car.

In America and Canada we call a "tender" a caboose, which is the end car on a train that carries supplies. Older translations either did not understand what a "tender" meant or translated it literally. Even if the older translators knew the meaning, readers, even readers of the 1930's did not know what it meant because it is a relatively obscure use of the word. Caboose is a US and Canadian term for the end train car which has supplies and sleeping areas for the crew. Tender is the car that carries fuel, water, and supplies and is the name used in Europe.

•

113

MEIN KAMPF

INACCURATE

Reynal-Hitchcock translation: Yet today this is so. Or, is it not ridiculous to try to drill, in the twilight of dawn, a regiment of some ten thousand men, although a few years previously

Murphy translation: It is not ridiculous to think of training some ten thousand men in the use of arms, and carry on that training surreptitiously, when a few years previously the State, having shamefully sacrificed eight-and-a-half million highly trained soldiers, not merely did not require their services any more, but, as a mark of gratitude for their sacrifices, held them up to public contumely.

CORRECT

Ford translation: It is ridiculous for an organization to even attempt to train some ten thousand men in the State's twilight of decline when, only a few years before, the State disgracefully abandoned eight and a half million men.

> The RH-translation says "twilight of dawn" which is not clear in context. This is because dawn indicates a beginning or a birth, which is contrary to the meaning of the passage which means a decline of the State. The Ford translation is correct when it says "twilight of decline". Murphy avoided the translation problem entirely by ignoring the reference so the twilight reference is not in his translation. If anything, the RH-translation should have been "twilight of dusk" because the decline was the important part, not the time of day so twilight itself means a period of decline and was adequate for an accurate translation in the case of the Ford translation.

INACCURATE

Reynal-Hitchcock translation: These were such sorry manifestations that at one time they caused the memorable late President Poehner, who in his hard straightforwardness hated all cringers as only a man with an honest heart is able to hate, to utter the harsh statement:...

Stackpole translation: These were such wretched figures that on one occasion they drove our unforgettable late President Pohner, who in his severe straightforwardness hated all fawning as only an honorable man can hate, to the blunt expression of opinion:...

CORRECT

MEIN KAMPF

Ford translation: These fake-nationalists were such terrible creatures that, on one occasion, they drove our unforgettable late Chief Pöhner to bluntly express his opinion.(Pöhner is Ernst Pöhner, the Bavarian Chief Of Police who was already mentioned in Volume 1; he died in a car accident in 1925 after his release from serving three months of a five year sentence for his part in the 1923 Putsch.) Chief Pöhner was critical in his straightforward manner and hated all such swindlers, as an honorable man should, he said, ...

> The original said *Prefect Pöhner,* who had already been discussed as the chief of police, he was not the President. The Ford translation is correct. It appears that neither of the other translators knew who the reference was actually about which is why they called him President here while he was already identified as Chief of Police earlier in Volume 1 even in their own translations. They thought the reference was to a leader and made it President, however that is not accurate.

INACCURATE

Reynal-Hitchcock translation: In these leagues tendencies of old war veteran associations and of the 'Kyffhauser' came to life and helped towards blunting the edge of the sharpest weapon which the national Germany of those days possessed, and towards letting it decay in the mercenary service of the Republic.
Murphy translation: The spirit of the old war legions and Kyffauser tendencies lived in them and therewith helped politically to blunt the sharpest weapons which the German nation then possessed and allow them to rust in the hands of republican serfs.

CORRECT

Ford translation: The militant defense units contained the spirit of the old soldiers and those who had faith in Kyffauser so they all looked towards the past fondly. (Kyffauser is a mountain range in Germany; there is a legend that Emperor Barbarossa sleeps in the mountain and will reawaken at a time of Germany's greatest need.)

> The RH-translation did not understand the meaning of Kyffauser. Murphy seemed to understand its placement in the sentence, but if he understood what it meant, he did not explain in the text

115

MEIN KAMPF

what it meant. The average English-language reader would not know what this reference meant. Only the Ford translation used it correctly and explained what it meant. The Ford translation is much longer, but the elaboration was necessary to fully explain what was being said in English.

INACCURATE

Reynal-Hitchcock translation: State power can guarantee quiet and order only if the State, according to its essentials, is identical with the currently prevalent view of life, so that brutal elements have merely the character of individual, criminal natures, and are not looked upon as the representatives of an idea that is the extreme opposite to the viewpoints of the State. In such a case the State may for centuries apply the strongest means of power against a terror by which it is threatened, but in the end it will be powerless, it will succumb.

Murphy translation: The rulers of the State can guarantee tranquillity and order only in case the State embodies a WELTANSCHAUUNG which is shared in by the people as a whole; so that elements of disturbance can be treated as isolated criminals, instead of being considered as the champions of an idea which is diametrically opposed to official opinions. If such should be the case the State may employ the most violent measures for centuries long against the terror that threatens it; but in the end all these measures will prove futile, and the State will have to succumb.

Stackpole translation: Likewise it is the eternal experience of world history that a terror represented by a world-concept never can be broken by a formal state authority but always succumbs only to a new and different world-concept, equally bold and determined. This will always be unpleasant to the official guardians of the state although this does not alter the fact in the least. State authority can guarantee peace and order only when the state and the ruling world-concept agree, so that violent elements possess only the character of individual criminal natures and are not considered as representatives of a purpose extremely opposed to the views of the state. In such a case the state can apply for centuries the most violent measures against a terror threatening it; in the end, however, the state will succumb being unable to accomplish anything against it.

CORRECT

Ford translation: State authority can guarantee peace and order only when the state world-concept and the world-concept of the people

MEIN KAMPF

agree. Violent elements promoting a world-concept, one that differs from the people's, will look like individual criminal groups and will not be seen as champions of an great idea which is opposed to the views of the state. If this were not the case, and the opposition held a world-concept that matched the people's world-concept, the state can apply the most violent measures for centuries against the terror threatening it, but, in the end, the state will submit because it is unable to defeat the opposing idea.

> The RH, Murphy, and Stackpole translations end with the last two sentences contradicting each other. First it says a state can successfully defend against violent world views and those promoting them will be seen as violent individuals, but then in the last sentence it contradicts the previous text and says the state cannot stand up against such a threat. So it says it can stand and then it says it can't. This appears to be a simple misinterpretation of the original German.
>
> The same error is in the Stackpole Translation. Only after a lot of review and consideration was this passage correctly re-translated in the Ford translation. The problem was in the previous translators attempts to tie the last sentence into the previous which was incorrect. They understood the individual sentences but missed the overall meaning. The "In such a case" part which all three translations share is the problem.
> It should have been translated as "If such were not the case" which would yield a consistent meaning.

INACCURATE

> **Murphy translation:** This idea was proved correct during the days from November 7 to 10, 1918. The Marxists did not then bother themselves in the least about parliament or democracy, but they gave the death blow to both by turning loose their horde of criminals to shoot and raise hell.
> **Reynal-Hitchcock translation:** How correct this conception is was proved in the days from November 7 to November 11, 1918. In those days Marxism did not care in the least for parliamentarianism and democracy, but it rendered both of them the deathblow by shouting and shooting gangs of criminals. It is a matter of course that the organizations of bourgeois babblers were defenseless at the same moment.

117

MEIN KAMPF

CORRECT

Ford translation: Marxism always held the point of view that weapons are to be used if they are expedient and success justified the use of arms. The accuracy of this point of view was demonstrated in the days from the November 7 to 11, 1918. At that time, Marxism didn't care at all for parliament or democracy and killed them both through howling and gun firing criminal gangs. The privileged-class chatter-boxes were defenseless in this moment.

> Murphy's translation had the wrong date of Nov 10. It should have been Nov 11. We also see that Murphy dropped the last line of this paragraph.

INACCURATE

Reynal-Hitchcock translation: A revolution has been made by a minority of the worst elements, backed immediately by the entire Marxist parties.
The revolution itself is of an apparently moderate character, a fact that draws upon it the hostility of the fanatical extremists.
Murphy translation: A minority constituted of the worst elements had made the Revolution. And behind this minority all the Marxist parties immediately fell into step. The Revolution itself had an outward appearance of moderation, which aroused against it the enmity of the fanatical extremists.

CORRECT

Ford translation: The Revolution was carried out by a minority of the worst elements, which all the Marxist parties immediately supported. The Revolution then stamped itself so that it appeared as moderate, which aroused the hostility of the fanatic extremists. The extremists began to throw around hand grenades and to fire off machine guns, occupying public buildings, and generally threatening the moderate Revolution.

> The time progression is important in Hitler's thought. Unfortunately this progress is not in the RH-translation or Murphy's translation. Hitler was giving an example of the progression of events and this first line was important in establishing that. The other translations do not make it clear that we are discussing a sequence of events whose order is important. The old translations relate the sentence as a series of facts, the revolution was carried out, it was backed by Marxists, it was

MEIN KAMPF

moderate. This loses the original meaning. The passage means the revolution was carried out and all of the Marxist parties supported it, then the revolution changed to a moderate appearance which alienated the extreme elements. The true meaning is lost in the old translations.

INACCURATE

Reynal-Hitchcock translation: then the unreliable man, becoming uncertain, cannot be held by threatening him with prison or even penal servitude....
Stackpole translation: Here threats of jail or prison sentence are of no value, for he knows from experience that in such times jail, or even prison, is many times safer than the battlefield, ...
Murphy Translation: ..often very badly supplied with food, the man who is unsure of himself and begins to waver cannot be made to stick to his post by threats of imprisonment or even penal servitude.

CORRECT

Ford translation: Threats of prison or even hard labor mean nothing to him

Neither of the older translators understood penal servitude which was created by German-English word substitution. It means hard labor. The Stackpole translation says jail or prison, but the statement does not make sense in Stackpole's version. Jail is generally local as in a city or county and short term. Prison is longer term and usually associated with a state-province or national justice system. It does not make sense to say "jail or prison" because no one would serve time in a local city jail resulting from their failure to serve in the military. That was not what the original German said. Again, the Ford translation is correct here.

INACCURATE

Reynal-Hitchcock translation: But that during the War one practically abolished the death penalty, that is that actually one put the Articles of War out of force, has taken its most terrible revenge.
Stackpole translation: It was a bad mistake to eliminate practically the

119

MEIN KAMPF

death penalty during the War, to call in the Articles of War, so to speak.
Murphy translation: The practical abolition of the death penalty during the war was a mistake for which we had to pay dearly.

CORRECT

Ford translation: It was a terrible mistake to eliminate the death penalty during a time of War and to initiate the Articles of War.

> The RH-translation incorrectly says the *articles of war was put out of force,* but this is not accurate. The articles of war were ***enacted*** which put the death penalty, which already existed, ***out of force***. This is another example of a mistranslation that completely changes the meaning of the text and causes confusion because it conflicts with statements elsewhere.
> Stackpole got it right though in a clumsy way, Murphy omitted the reference to the Articles of War in this sentence completely to avoid the translation problem which also made the sentence very generic in his translation.

INACCURATE

Reynal-Hitchcock translation: For the voluntary war hero, of course, no Articles of War were necessary, but for the cowardly egoist who in the hour
of his people's distress evaluates his life higher than that of the community.

Murphy translation: For the voluntary war hero it is, of course, not necessary to have the death penalty in the military code, but it is necessary for the cowardly egoists who value their own lives more than the existence of the community in the hour of national need.
Stackpole translation: Of course, no Articles of War were necessary for the heroes who volunteered; they were needed for the cowardly egotist, who, in the hour of his people's need, values his life higher than that of his country.

CORRECT

Ford translation: The hero who volunteered needed no threats of the death penalty.

MEIN KAMPF

Stackpole and Reynal confused the reference. It was to the death penalty, not The Articles Of War. The Articles of war did NOT call for a death penalty and that was Hitler's complaint. He thought they *should* call for the death penalty. So it was not what was being referred to in the sentence, yet they both translated the generic reference(it) as referring to Articles Of War and substituted the full name in an attempt to make it clearer. It is clearly incorrect when looking at the meaning of the sentence and the surrounding sentences. The Murphy and Ford translations correctly translated the passage.

INACCURATE

Reynal-Hitchcock translation: ...in the year 1918, flooded the military base and the home country and helped towards forming that great and criminal organization which,...

Murphy translation: An army of deserters poured into the stations at the rear or returned home, especially in 1918, and there began to form that huge criminal...

Stackpole translation: Especially in 1918, an army of deserters gushed forth, both in the troops, behind the line, and at home, and helped form that large, destructive organization which we suddenly saw before us as the makers of the Revolution after November 7, 1918.

CORRECT

Ford translation: When they were passed, in 1918, an army of deserters erupted from the troops, filling the military prisons that were safely behind the lines, and many took trains to return home.

Note how older translations missed the reference to military prisons. Reynal simply said 'military base', Murphy said station, Stackpole Translation said 'behind the line', none understood the actual translation meant military prisons. It makes no sense that a deserter would go back to basecamp just to sit around, if he did then he would be put in prison anyway.

The Ford translation does add the word trains which was implied but not in the original however it is only logical since that is the only transport available that could have taken them home.

MEIN KAMPF

Stackpole Translation Example

>...and should thoroughly examine the situation before enlarging its organization.
>{Page Break}
>before enlarging its organization. Only by such means will it be able to keep the nucleus of the movement...

This is a page break in the Stackpole Translation. You can see how the text was carried over from page to page. This indicates it was rushed to press before it was ready. They had to rush because they knew the publication might be stopped for copyright reasons. The result was a very sloppy translation with many similar errors.

INACCURATE

>**Reynal-Hitchcock translation:** or, as the bourgeois world usually says quite correctly in such a case: 'The wine has been mixed with water.' And then, indeed, the trees can no longer grow up to the heavens
>**Murphy translation:** The fire of the first fervour died out, the fighting spirit flagged and, as the bourgeois world is accustomed to say very justly in such cases, the party mixed water with its wine. For this reason it is necessary that a movement should, from the sheer instinct of self-preservation, close its lists to new membership the...

CORRECT

>**Ford translation:** The fanatical goal has been erased from their minds, the fighting strength becomes crippled, or as the privileged-class world would rightly say in such cases: "Water has been mixed with the wine." When this happens, indeed, the trees can no longer grow up to heaven.

>>Here the Murphy translation skipped a line about the largest tree. It was not uncommon for him to reword passages and drop parts that no longer fit his rewording.

INACCURATE

>**Stackpole translation:** And added to that: Not only the best extreme became thinned on the battlefield in the most monstrous way for four and a half years, but the worst, in the meantime, in the most remarkable

way were conserved. To be sure on every volunteer hero climbing the steps to Valhalla by the holy death of sacrifice, fell a poltroon who very cautiously turned his back to death in order to give practical proof of his being more or less useful in the homeland in their stead.

CORRECT

Ford translation: The hostile, vile, and cowardly elements in this mass of the worst extreme became dominant. Add to that the fact that not only did the best extreme group become thinned out on the battlefield in the most horrible way, for four and a half years, but the worst group was protected in the most remarkable way. For every volunteer hero who climbed the steps to Valhalla by their holy sacrifice of death, there was a wretched coward who very cautiously turned his back on death so he could prove his usefulness in the homeland by taking the place of the volunteers now serving in battle.

> This is a common example of the Stackpole Translation method. Much of it is a direct substitution-translation which is made without understanding of the original material. The complexities of the original German are preserved almost exactly which makes if very confusing. There are countless errors in pronouns and clauses which are collected together in such a way that they refer to ideas they were not meant to refer to or the long series of *he/him/them*'s make it impossible to tell who is doing what.

Another Example of this:

INACCURATE

Stackpole translation: One realizes this by recognizing all the sacrifice of the intermediate class, which lead to an almost complete blood-letting of the best men. And what was shed of the irreplaceable blood of German heroes in these four and a half years, is monstrous. One adds up all the hundred thousand particulars.

Here the second sentence makes no sense in context.

Another Example:

INACCURATE

Stackpole translation: But one considers before everything that the year 1914 with the whole army made up of so-called volunteers who, thanks to the criminal unscrupulousness of our parliamentary do-nothings, had obtained no valid, perfecting peace, and so now had surrendered like defenceless cannon-fodder to the enemy.

Reynal-Hitchcock translation: But one should consider above all that the year 1914 put up entire armies of so-called volunteers who, thanks to the criminal lack of conscience of our parliamentary good-for-nothings, had not been given an efficient peace-time training, and who thus now, as defenseless cannon fodder, were exposed to the enemy.

Murphy translation: In 1914 whole armies were composed of volunteers who, owing to a criminal lack of conscience on the part of our feckless parliamentarians, had not received any proper training in times of peace, and so were thrown as defenceless cannon-fodder to the enemy.

CORRECT

Ford translation: The most important thing to consider is that in 1914, the whole army was made up of volunteers who, thanks to the criminal corruption of our parliamentary do-nothings, had received no real peace-time training for war and were handed over to the enemy as defenseless men.

The Stackpole Translation translates *perfecting peace.* This is not in the original German text. It should have said *peacetime military training*. The RH, Murphy and Ford translations are correct. However, only the Ford translation is both accurate and easy to understand.

INACCURATE

Murphy translation: The controversy over federation and unification, so cunningly propagandized by the Jews in 1919-1920 and onwards,
Reynal-Hitchcock translation: The fight so slyly propagated by the Jews between federalism and centralization in the years 1919-20-21 and thereafter,...

CORRECT

Ford translation: The dispute between federalism(strong state level government) and a nationalism(strong national centralized government), which was propagated by the Jews in such a cunning way during the years 1919-1921, compelled the National Socialist

MEIN KAMPF

movement,...

> The date in Murphy's translation was incorrect and again we see the consistent problem with unclear terminology when it comes to state-government vs national-government interests which are shown in the older translations as unification or centralization which have different meanings themselves. Only the Ford translation is both correct and understandable.

INACCURATE

Murphy translation: Ought Germany to be a confederacy or a military State?
Reynal-Hitchcock translation: Should Germany be a federated State or a unified State, and what does each mean practically?

CORRECT

Ford translation: Should Germany be a confederation of states or one national central government?

> Murphy thought Hitler was proposing a military state, however the discussion this came from was *state versus national central government* and not military government. The translation is simply wrong. Reynal is correct and the Ford translation is both correct and easily understood.

INACCURATE

Reynal-Hitchcock translation: Accordingly, there remained no split-up whatsoever from this first time of the movement, but the honest intentions of the men of those days nearly throughout led to an honest, straight and correct end.
Murphy translation: When that first period of the movement was over there remained no further dispersion of forces: for their honest intentions had led the men of that time to the same honourable, straightforward and just conclusion.

CORRECT

Ford translation: No division remains from these early days of the movement. The honest will and intent of those men led almost without

MEIN KAMPF

exception to an honorable, upright, and proper outcome.

> Murphy misunderstood the meaning of *division* and thought it meant a dispersion of forces, when it actually meant a division or conflict between merging groups.

INACCURATE

Reynal-Hitchcock translation: By a workers' community one generally understands a group of associations which, in order to facilitate their common work, enter into a certain mutual relationship, choose a common leader of more or less great competence and carry out common actions in common.
Murphy translation: In speaking of a co-operative union we generally mean a group of associations which, for the purpose of facilitating their work, establish mutual relations for collaborating with one another along certain lines, appointing a common directorate with varying powers and thenceforth carrying out a common line of action.

CORRECT

Ford translation: They chose a common leadership of lesser or greater authority and plan things together.

> The RH translation mistakenly thought *greater/lesser* referred to the competence of the leadership but it actually referred to the higher and lower rank of the leaders as shown by the Ford translation and Murphy's translation.

INACCURATE

Murphy translation: There I had the chance of seeing what a bourgeois meeting could be.
Reynal-Hitchcock translation: I should have liked to see a bourgeois meeting under such circumstances!

CORRECT

Ford translation: I would have liked to have seen a privileged-class meeting in that situation!

> This describes a disturbance at a National Socialist meeting and Hitler's statement that he would have liked to have seen

MEIN KAMPF

that kind passion at a bourgeois(privileged-class) meeting, however Murphy's translation appears to say Hitler was looking at what a bourgeois meeting could be as if he were impressed or approving which makes no sense in context. Hitler was putting down bourgeois meetings, not analyzing their potential or complementing them. It is likely Murphy understood the passage, but the way it is worded is not as clear as it could be in his translation.

INACCURATE

Murphy translation: ??????????? MISSING ???????????????

CORRECT

Ford translation: If these kinds of things were done by others, it was the Marxists' holy right to consider it a provocation because, until now, they were the sole owners of this monopoly.

Murphy omitted this sentence, as well as others, completely.

INACCURATE

Murphy translation: Even the arena was densely crowded.
Reynal-Hitchcock translation: Even the arena was black with crowds.

CORRECT

Ford translation: The center of the arena was so filled that it appeared black with spectators.

Here Murphy omitted the "black with crowds" part and oversimplified it while in other areas he embellishes heavily which removes Hitler's style.

If one word is changed, it is not a big deal but when you change a word here and another there, then elaborate in one area but not another, the original style is lost. Hitler's style is important because this style is what listeners heard at his speeches. This is the style that moved them emotionally and made them want to follow him. When the style is lost, Hitler is lost and it becomes a jumble of words.

MEIN KAMPF

INACCURATE

Murphy translation: ...its effect at that time was something akin to that of a blazing torch.
Reynal-Hitchcock translation: No one had ever seen it before; in those days it had an effect like that of a flaming torch

CORRECT

Ford translation: No one had ever seen it before and its effect was like a firebrand(a person who stirs up trouble or kindles a revolution).

Both translations use *flaming torch* but the original German was closer to firebrand which is not a torch, but a person who stirs up revolution and this fits the paragraph much better than to give a predictable and generic comparison to a burning torch. Some of the meaning was lost in the older translations which has been restored in the Ford translation. Also this says the effect was like a firebrand, which was not talking about how it looked which would be a torch. Torch does not fit. Firebrand is the correct translation.

INACCURATE

Reynal-Hitchcock translation: ...approached my own design very closely, except that it had the one mistake that the swastika was composed in a white circle with curved hooks.

CORRECT

Ford translation: It was a lot like mine, but had the one flaw, the swastika, it had curved ends and was inside a thin white circle.

Reynal chose the word *mistake* which was a word substitution translation. A more accurate word is *flaw*. No one can design an artistic creation and make a "mistake" however if they are designing for someone else, it can have a flaw in that person's opinion. Therefore the use of the word mistake was itself a mistake and an inaccurate translation. A series of such mistakes can alter the meaning of a sentence, make it softer than it was intended, make it harsher than intended, and even change the meaning entirely in some cases.

MEIN KAMPF

INACCURATE

Reynal-Hitchcock translation: ..this, then, was fired with quite a different material; the press.
Murphy translation: The engine was heated with quite different stuff: namely, the journalistic Press.

CORRECT

Ford translation: The Jewish machine itself was fired by a different fuel, the press.

> The older translations misunderstood the meaning of the sentence. It is not clear what the older translations mean. In the Ford translation the meaning is clear. It meant fuel. Hitler was saying the Jewish machine was fueled by the press.

INACCURATE

Reynal-Hitchcock translation: The case is quite different with the 'spoken' leaflet !
Murphy translation: It is quite different with the 'spoken' leaflet.

CORRECT

Ford translation: The leaflet for a speech is different matter.

> The older translations are literal but have no meaning. What is a spoken-leaflet? The original German meant a leaflet advertising a public speech and not a spoken leaflet. Both older translators missed the meaning and opted for a straight word for word translation. Fortunately it is corrected in the Ford translation.

INACCURATE

Murphy translation: I myself was always for keeping the old colours, not only because I, as a soldier, regarded them as my most sacred possession, but because in their aesthetic effect, they conformed more than anything else to my personal taste.
Reynal-Hitchcock translation: I personally always stood up for keeping the old colors, not only because to me, as a soldier, they are the most sacred thing I know, but also, because of their aesthetic effect,

129

MEIN KAMPF

they correspond to my feeling by far to the greatest extent.

CORRECT

Ford translation: I was inclined to retain the colors of the old flag because they are the most sacred thing to me as a soldier and also because their aesthetic effect appeals far more than any other to my artistic sense.

> Murphy changed the translation heavily and completely omitted the artistic references which were important because Hitler was an artist. This passage describes to the design of the Nazi flag and we see the same problem in the RH-translation. The word artistic was important here and is included in the Ford translation.

INACCURATE

Murphy translation: For this reason we declined all suggestions from various quarters for identifying our movement by means of a white flag with the old State or rather with those decrepit parties whose sole political objective is the restoration of past conditions. And, apart from this, white is not a colour capable of attracting and focusing public attention. It is a colour suitable only for young women's associations and not for a movement that stands for reform in a revolutionary period.

Reynal-Hitchcock translation: For this reason we had to reject all suggestions for identifying by a white flag, as was suggested from many sides, our movement with the old State or rather with those weak parties whose sole interest is the restoration of past conditions. Apart from this, white is not a color that carries people away. It is suitable for associations of chaste virgins, but not for the overpowering movement of a revolutionary time.

CORRECT

Ford translation: For this reason, we had to decline the suggestion that we use a white flag. That recommendation came from many areas. A white flag would have surely identified our movement with the old State and with those feeble parties whose sole political aim is to restore the old Empire. Besides, white is not a compelling color. It is suitable for innocent societies of maidens, but not for rebellious movements in a revolutionary age.

MEIN KAMPF

Murphy missed the joke and tried to make white flag something relating to the old state flag of Germany. Hitler was actually telling a joke by saying that opponent political groups suggested he wave the white flag of surrender. The Reynal translation is technically accurate but the joke was lost in the translation here too. Only the Ford translation relates what Hitler was trying to say with humor.

There were actually a series of jokes here. First he rejects the white flag then he says it was identified with the old state which is a jab at the old state for surrendering in World War I and surrendering to the Marxists. When Hitler says *suitable for women*, he is not being serious as such, though the color was common in women's dresses of the day, he is acting like he is seriously considering it when he is not. Hitler takes the jest of a white flag and in the last sentence turns it around and uses it to remind people of the power of the Nazi movement. This is a very clever twist. He uses a joke made by his opponents to drive home a point of his own.

INACCURATE

Reynal-Hitchcock translation: One needed them at least for a certain time, and only after the Moors had done their duty could one dare to give them the kick they deserved and to take the Republic
Stackpole translation: They were still needed for a time at least, and not until the Moors had done their duty could one venture to give them the kick they deserved,
Murphy translation: They would be needed at least for a certain time, and only when they had served the purpose of Turks' Heads could the deserved kick-out be administered with impunity.

CORRECT

Ford translation: Only after the old officials had served their purpose as Turk's Heads and had done their duty could the revolutionaries risk giving them the kick they deserved and take the Republic out of the hands of the old servants of the State and deliver it to the claws of the revolutionary vultures. (*Turk's Head is a type of decorative knot; here it means the government officials were kept as decoration.*)

> The RH and Stackpole translations mistranslated the Turk's Head reference as Moors. Turk's Head is a type of fancy decorative knot which might be known to a soldier. Murphy may not have recognized the meaning, but he translated it accurately. Only the Ford translation was technically accurate and explained what the reference meant.

131

MEIN KAMPF

INACCURATE

>**Murphy translation:** if there was any resistance, to break it with trench-mortars and hand grenades,
>**Stackpole translation:** up against the wall and to break down any possible opposition with trench-mortars and hand-grenades, this division would ...
>**Reynal-Hitchcock translation:** For if in those days only one single division commander had come to the decision to pull down, with the help of the division loyally devoted to him, the red rags and to have the 'Councils' stood up against the wall, and to break eventual resistance with mine-throwers and hand grenades, then this division would have swelled up to an army of sixty divisions in less than four weeks.

CORRECT

>**Ford translation:**...had decided to pull down the Red rag with the division loyal to him and to stand the Revolution leaders up against the wall and to break down any possible opposition with trench-mortars and hand-grenades, this division...

>>The RH-translation mistranslated *mine-thrower*. Of course, mines are not thrown. Another example of technical translation without understanding the meaning. The Murphy, Ford and Stackpole translations were correct.

INACCURATE

>**Murphy translation:** (2) An organized squad of troops to maintain order.

This corrected line was not included in the original German volume 2 and it was is not in the Ford translation because it was not in the original German. This is an example of how Murphy 'corrected' the original text by adding a number 2 when there was originally no number 2. The original text began enumerating but missed the second item; Murphy added it *for* Hitler.

MEIN KAMPF

INACCURATE

Murphy translation: At meetings, particularly outside Munich, we had in those days from five to eight hundred opponents against fifteen to sixteen National Socialists; yet we brooked no interference, for we were ready to be killed rather than capitulate.

CORRECT

Ford translation: Our opponents knew that anyone who dared to incite trouble would be harshly thrown out, even though we might be a dozen against five hundred. In the meetings at that time, particularly outside of Munich, there would be fifteen or sixteen National-Socialists to five, six, seven, or eight hundred opponents.

Murphy said five to eight hundred, instead of listing individual numbers. This changed the striking speech style of Hitler which he used to build to a stronger emotional plateau. The Ford translation makes a stronger effort to preserve all of his nuances as much as possible in a translation.

INACCURATE

Reynal-Hitchcock translation: But if, as an exception, such a position was held by a genuine German official, not an official creature, and if he rejected the impudent demands, then there followed the notorious appeal not to tolerate such a 'provocation of the proletariat' but to appear in masses at a meeting, on such and such a date, in order to 'put a stop to the disgraceful activity of the bourgeois creatures with the help of the horny fist of the proletarian.'

Murphy translation: If by chance the official happened to be a true German--and not a mere figurehead--and he declined the impudent request, then the time-honoured appeal to stop 'provocation of the proletariat' was issued together with instructions to attend such and such a meeting on a certain date in full strength for the purpose of 'putting a stop to the disgraceful machinations of the bourgeoisie by means of the proletarian fist'.

CORRECT

Ford translation: However, if the official's post was occupied, for once, by a real German civil servant rather than just a political creature filling an office seat and he refused such an offensive and bold request, the result would be the familiar appeal to their party members not to

133

MEIN KAMPF

tolerate such a "provocation of the working class," but to attend the meeting in a large group on the scheduled date and to "put an end to the shameful plot by privileged-class creatures using the calloused fist of the working class."

Neither Murphy nor Reyanl correctly translate *Callused*. Murphy skipped it and Reynal incorrectly translated it as *Horny* which gives a totally different meaning.

INACCURATE

Reynal-Hitchcock translation: How did not many a one, upon entering our meeting, shout this sentence boastingly to another one, in order to find himself, even before he could shout it a second time, outside the entrance of the hall.
Murphy translation: How often did they bawl this out to each other on entering the meeting hall, only to be thrown out with lightning speed before they had time to repeat it.

CORRECT

Ford translation: Many of them yelled this boast as they walked into our meeting, but immediately, he found himself sitting outside the entrance to the hall before he could interrupt a second time.

The RH-translation is hard to read "*how did not many a one*". The Ford translation and Murphy are easier to understand. Many passages in RH as well as Manheim are choppy like this and hard to understand.

INACCURATE

Reynal-Hitchcock translation:...and not infrequently one had the impression as
though he were even grateful to Fate for the quick abbreviation of the torturing procedure.
Murphy translation: One gathered the impression at times that these speakers were graceful for being peremptorily cut short in their martyr-like discourse.

CORRECT

Ford translation: Often, one had the impression that he was even grateful to Fate for cutting short the agonizing process.

MEIN KAMPF

Murphy removed the reference to Fate and inserted "martyr-like" which was not in the original German text. Reynal and Ford translated the passage correctly.

The following is based on this

Ford translation: Therefore, he requested that the speaker be allowed to finish his remarks, which he assured the crowd would not be very much longer, so the world would not see again any shameful display of bad blood between German brothers. Ugh!

INACCURATE

Murphy translation: And so on and so forth
Reynal-Hitchcock translation: ugh
Stackpole translation: Brrr!

CORRECT

Ford translation: Ugh!

Murphy omitted the *Ugh*, which means an expression of horror, disgust or repugnance. In removing this expression of emotion he removed some of Hitler's style from the document. Murphy either mistook the interjection for an alternative of *etc*, which Hitler was font of, and replaced it with his sentence which is not in the original or simply ignored it.

INACCURATE

Murphy translation: Therefore, the way in which men are generally esteemed by their fellow-citizens must not be according to the kind of work they do, because that has been more or less assigned to the individual.
Reynal-Hitchcock translation: For this work comes on account of his birth and of the training conditioned by it which he received from the community.

CORRECT

Ford translation: Consequently, one's social position should not force a job on the individual. His job should be attributed to his abilities at birth and to the education the community has provided to him.

135

MEIN KAMPF

Murphy's sentence implies someone should not be judged by the work they do because they were assigned a job, however the meaning of the paragraph was that the person *should not* be assigned a job based on social position but on ability. The Murphy translation does not match the original meaning.

INACCURATE

Reynal-Hitchcock translation: The N.S.G.W.P. must not become a bailiff of public opinion, but its ruler.
Murphy translation: The National Socialist German Labour Party ought not to be the beadle but rather the master of public opinion.

CORRECT

Ford translation: The NSDAP must not be a follower of public opinion, but must become the master of public opinion.

The original meaning of this passage was intended to be more of an escort or an usher however usher is open to interpretation and escort has alternate common meanings which would have obscured the real meaning of the passage. The word was made *follower* which is closer to the true meaning in the Ford translation.
The word *beadle* means a minor parish official like a church usher in Murphy's translation, however the average English speaker would not recognize this word. The word *bailiff* which is used in the RH translation is not accurate.

INACCURATE

Murphy translation: But the real author of the Revolution and of the process of disintegration in the Army was not the soldier who had fought at the front but the CANAILLE which more or less shunned the light and which were either quartered in the home garrisons or were officiating as 'indispensables' somewhere in the business world at home.
Reynal-Hitchcock translation: ...of the army not the front soldier, but the more or less light-shunning rabble that either loitered about in the home garrisons or that served somewhere, as 'indispensable' in the economic service.

136

MEIN KAMPF

CORRECT

Ford translation: This deterioration was not caused by the soldiers at the front. This was the work of the riff-raff, that lowest group, that hid from the light and spent their time either loafing around in home-based military garrisons or working in the homeland somewhere because they were "unfit" for duty.

> The end of the passage is a sarcastic jab calling the riff-raff group "indispensable" or that they wanted to make themselves appear as if they were indispensable. Both older translations say "indispensable", but the Ford translation makes more sense and matches the original German.

INACCURATE

Reynal-Hitchcock translation: With such a movement one is no longer faced by an active extreme, but by the great masses of the middle, that is, inertia.
Murphy translation: If such a movement were attempted the leaders would find that it was not an extreme section of the population on which they had to depend but rather the broad masses of the middle stratum; hence the inert masses.
Stackpole translation: In such a movement one no longer has an extreme of activity before him, but the broad inactive mass of the middle, and a burden of inactivity.

CORRECT

Ford translation: When a movement reaches this stage, it is no longer a group from the extreme of the population, but contains the broad mass of the middle group which is nothing more than a burden because they are inactive.

> The RH version translated *inertia* which does not make sense in the sentence. The true meaning was an inert, unmoving group. RH opted for the literal translation and not the underlying meaning. The other translations were correct. The Ford translation was the easiest to understand and it is also closer to the original German wording which used "burden".

MEIN KAMPF

INACCURATE

Murphy translation: What can be said of persons who debased themselves so far, for the sake of a little abject praise in the Jewish Press, that they persecuted those men to whose heroic courage and intervention, regardless of risk, they were partly indebted for not having been torn to pieces by the Red mob a few years previously and strung up to the lamp-posts?

Reynal-Hitchcock translation: What was one to say to men who in their self-abasement went so far as to persecute, for the wretched praise of Jewish papers, those men to whose heroic staking of their lives they in part owed it that a few years previously their maimed corpses had not been hung up on lampposts by the red mob?

CORRECT

Ford translation: These people were so disgraceful that, in exchange for the miserable praise of Jewish newspapers, they did not hesitate to persecute the very men whose heroic intervention they should have thanked in part for their own lives; it was these men who prevented their mutilated corpses from being hanged from light-posts by the Red jackals only a few years ago.

Murphy cleaned up the original text in the last line by leaving out graphic words. In the Ford translation it says jackals. The original German word actually should be *pack,* but the word by itself is unclear. The meaning was more accurately *a pack of dogs*, but *a pack of dogs* was too wordy to substitute so jackals was used. It conveys the meaning without being too wordy.

INACCURATE

Reynal-Hitchcock translation: but because it understood that the greatest spirit can be eliminated if its bearer is slain by the rubber truncheon, as actually in history the most important minds not infrequently ended under the blows of smallest helots.

Stackpole translation: but because these men understood that the highest ideal can be exterminated if its leader is killed by a rubber blackjack.

Murphy translation: They used the cudgel because they knew that it can be made impossible for high ideals to be put forward if the man who endeavours to propagate them can be struck down with the cudgel.

MEIN KAMPF

CORRECT

Ford translation: However, it did not regard the rubber billy-club as the highest ideal as some stupid German nationalists claimed, but these men understood that the highest ideal can be exterminated if its leader is knocked low by a rubber billy-club.

The RH version translates "slain" by a rubber truncheon. The actual word in German more accurately means knocked down, not slain. There is a big difference between those two meanings. One means killed and the other does not. Also note that the correct translation is rubber club however Murphy shortened it to cudgel which implies a wooden nightstick which was not used. Again, there is a big difference between hitting someone on the head with a rubber baton and a wooden baton so this totally changes the meaning. Reynal was correct. The Ford translation was also correct but club was extended to billy club in the Ford translation to make the meaning even clearer and to avoid confusion by possible alternate meanings of *club*.

INACCURATE

Murphy translation: In the autumn, or rather in the spring, of 1919 it was still possible to raise 'volunteer corps',
Reynal-Hitchcock translation: In the fall, or rather still in the spring, of 1919 it was possible to establish so-called ' Free Corps,'

CORRECT

Ford translation: In the fall, and more so in the spring, of 1919 it was possible to organize "volunteer corps."

Murphy translated the passage as "in autumn or rather in the spring" which is not accurate. Such translation errors make Hitler look scatterbrained which was not the case. Hitler is not confused about the time. The Ford translation is the most correct translation which shows a progression, first the autumn, then more so in the spring. Hitler liked to use progressions like this.
Reynal incorrectly translated Free Corps, which was a militant organization and not associated with the SA Storm Troops. It was the SA Storm Troops which were actually being discussed, not the Free Corps. RH confused "volunteer corps" as a general descriptive term with the translation as the name of the militant organization by the same/similar name, Free Corps.

MEIN KAMPF

INACCURATE

> **Reynal-Hitchcock translation:** Entirely through their own complicity.
> **Murphy translation:** They were the victims of their own defaults.
> **Stackpole translation:** Seldom did Heaven's judgment follow the act of sinning as rapidly as in this case. The same parties which only a few years previously had placed the interest of their own states above the interests of the Reich-this was particularly the case in Bavaria-were now compelled to witness the throttling of the existence of the individual states by the interests of the Reich, which situation was brought about by the pressure of events.

CORRECT

> **Ford translation:** They brought these events on themselves.

Which of these sentences makes the most sense? Only the Ford translation is understandable, either in context or as a standalone sentence. The older translations used mechanical translation here which is basic word substitution. The meaning is lost in the older translations. Here, Hitler used another saying that is common in both English and German but none of the old translations recognized it.

Here is another example from the same paragraph(this one is first in the paragraph):

INACCURATE

> **Reynal-Hitchcock translation:** Avenging history!
> **Stackpole translation:** Avenging history!
> **Murphy translation:** The retribution of History!

CORRECT

> **Ford translation:** Time avenges all!

Reynal and Stackpole translate directly without understanding the meaning in context. Murphy understands the meaning better but becomes hung up on the word *history* which in this sense meant time. The Ford translation was the most correct and it is the only one that is understandable. It could have been translated as History Avenges All! but in English history means the past and in this context the meaning was time not history. The meaning is lost in the older translations. Here, Hitler used another saying that is common in both English and German but none of the old translations recognized it.

MEIN KAMPF

INACCURATE

Reynal-Hitchcock translation: To complain to the voting masses (for the agitation of our contemporary parties is directed only towards them) about the loss of die individual States' sovereign rights, while all these parties without exception overbid each other in a policy of fulfillment whose final consequences naturally had to lead also to profound alterations in internal Germany, is matchless hypocrisy.

Stackpole translation: It is an unparalleled hypocrisy towards the electorate (with which alone the agitation of our present parties is concerned) to deplore the loss of sovereignty by different states, while at the same time these very parties endeavored to outbid each other in pursuing a fulfillment policy, the consequences of which were bound to lead to far-reaching internal changes in Germany.

Murphy translation: But these parties, without exception, outbid one another in accepting a policy of fulfilment which, by the sheer force of circumstances and in its ultimate consequences, could not but lead to a profound alteration in the internal structure of the REICH.

CORRECT

Ford translation: It is an unbelievable hypocrisy for the representatives of the different states to complain about the loss of their sovereignty in front of the voting masses, which is the only place our flustered parties direct anything, while at the same time these very parties tried to out-do each other in pursuing a policy of fulfillment, to fulfill the payment terms resulting from the Treaty of Versailles, when it was clear even then that the consequences of this payment would lead to far-reaching internal changes in Germany.

The old translations merely mention *fulfillment*, but if you do know what it means then you cannot understand what is being discussed. Only the Ford translation trans makes the passage clear and understandable. It was necessary to add "*to fulfill the payment terms resulting from the Treaty of Versailles*" so the average reader would know what fulfillment was referring to.

141

MEIN KAMPF

INACCURATE

Murphy translation: They may retard but they cannot stop the revolutions of history.

CORRECT

Ford translation: There have been and always will be people who refuse to admit the obvious, but they cannot slow the "wheel of history" and they can certainly never stop it.

Murphy translated wheel as revolutions, but it should have been wheel which is in the original German. Murphy's translation can be misinterpreted to imply that he is speaking of a violent government overthrow type revolution but that is not the case at all in this sentence as shown by the correct Ford translation. He tried to say the revolutions as in the rotation of history, but considering the political meaning of revolutions and the political context of the book, it is too easily misunderstood here. Murphy's translation is correct if it is explained but confusing if it is not explained and could be taken to mean they cannot stop the government overthrows of history. It is possible Hitler intended both meanings at the same time too.

INACCURATE

Reynal-Hitchcock translation: Indeed, when one of their people really dared oppose this mad system seriously, he was outlawed and damned and hounded as 'not standing on the ground of the existing State,'...
Murphy translation: Indeed, when anyone seriously opposed the madness that was shown in carrying out this system of centralization he was told by those same parties that he understood nothing of the nature and needs of the State to-day.
Stackpole translation: But, if any man did dare seriously to oppose this crazy system, then the same parties would outlaw and condemn him as "one who is not in harmony with the present State,"...

CORRECT

Ford translation: But if anybody dared to seriously oppose this crazy system of centralization, the same parties would come forward and ostracize and condemn him as "someone who is not in touch with the current State."

The RH and Stackpole translations are hard to understand.

142

MEIN KAMPF

Murphy is close but only the Ford translation is both accurate and understandable. This is another common phrase, "not being in touch", which was missed by the older translations.

INACCURATE

Stackpole translation: The National-Socialist doctrine is not the servant of the political interests of individual federates states, but is to be ruler of the German nation. It has the life of a people to destine and to regulate anew, and therefore it must positively claim the right to ignore boundaries, drawn by evolutionary forces, which we reject.
Murphy translation: The National Socialist doctrine is not handmaid to the political interests of the single federal states. One day it must become teacher to the whole German nation. It must determine the life of the whole people and shape that life anew. For this reason we must imperatively demand the right to overstep boundaries that have been traced by a political development which we repudiate.
Reynal-Hitchcock translation: The National Socialist theory is not the servant of the political interests of individual federated States, but shall some day be the mistress of the German nation. It must determine and reorder the life of a nation, and therefore must imperiously demand for itself the right to overlook boundaries drawn by a tendency which we have rejected.

CORRECT

Ford translation: The National-Socialist idea must be just as unrestricted by state boundaries as the churches are unbound by political lines. The National-Socialist doctrine is not the servant of the individual state's political interests, but must dominate the German nation as a whole. It must guide the people to a new life and give them a destiny, therefore, it must claim the absolute right to ignore boundaries drawn by past political forces that we now reject.

Murphy was said teacher, but the original word was mistress which actually meant a nation that has supremacy over others, at least in this context. Reynal translated directly, however the meaning today is not the same as it was then and can also mean submissive as in a kept-woman, owner, or educated in a specific skill. Murphy likely misunderstood because in Britain, mistress can mean a female schoolteacher, which explains why he translated it as teacher.(James Murphy was British) However,

143

MEIN KAMPF

Murphy's translation was still incorrect because he misunderstood what he was translating here. The Ford translation is again the most correct.

We can also see how Murphy dropped a sentence. "*It must guide the people to a new life and give them a destiny, therefore,*" was dropped from his translation but is present in all others.

INACCURATE

Reynal-Hitchcock translation: This is all the more necessary today, since the young German no longer has as previously his wander-years with their broadening effect on his horizon.

CORRECT

Ford translation: Today, this is even more necessary since the young German does not travel to broaden his horizons as he once did.

The RH translation had a consistent problem of writing sentences in a very complex, unordered and difficult to understand manner. Here it is very hard to understand. Compare the RH to the Ford Translation which is easy to understand and very clear.

INACCURATE

Reynal-Hitchcock translation: I see it either in the field of tribal affairs or cultural policy.
Stackpole translation: The importance of the individual states will no longer lie in the state and the domain of power politics. I see it either in the regional domain or in the sphere of cultural politics.

CORRECT

Ford translation: This also holds an important lesson for our future. The importance of the individual states will no longer lie in the state's domain of political power. I see them as important ethnic and cultural centers.

The RH-translation misunderstood the German text and translated as "tribal affairs", but the passage is not talking about tribes at all. It means ethnic-affairs or as shown in the Ford translation, ethnic center, which is correct for its place in the sentence.

144

MEIN KAMPF

INACCURATE

Reynal-Hitchcock translation: ...who wanted, in her, to give the German nation an artistic gem which would have to be, and which was, respected and esteemed. And this holds a lesson for the future, too.
Murphy translation: What made this a city of importance was the King who wished to present it to the German nation as an artistic jewel that would have to be seen and appreciated, and so it has turned out in fact. Therein lies a lesson for the future.

CORRECT

Ford translation: Instead, the town became important through the efforts of the King(Ludwig I), who wanted to give the German nation a treasure of art that would have to be seen and appreciated. And that is exactly how it turned out. This also holds an important lesson for our future.

> The passage talks about how Ludwig I made Munich a great center of art and culture. You can see that the RH-translation passage makes no sense and it does not tie into any later sentence either. The Ford translation is correct. Murphy is also correct but unclear. Reynal actually took two sentences, the first word from one, dropped the rest and stuck the second sentence on the end omitting part of the meaning which is why the RH translation came out as it did.

INACCURATE

Murphy translation: In the years 1920-21 the movement was controlled by a committee elected by the members at a general meeting. The committee was composed of a first and second treasurer, a first and second secretary, and a first and second chairman at the head of it. In addition to these there was a representative of the members, the director of propaganda, and various assessors.
Reynal-Hitchcock translation: During the years 1919 to 1920 the movement had as its leaders a committee which was elected by meetings of members, which in turn were prescribed by the by-laws. The committee consisted of a first and a second treasurer, a first and a second secretary, and as their head a first and a second chairman. To this were added the membership secretaries, the chief of propaganda, and various additional committeemen.

MEIN KAMPF

CORRECT

Ford translation: From 1919 to 1920, the movement was led by a committee which was elected by the members in special assemblies as detailed in our rules. The committee consisted of a first and second treasurer, a first and second secretary, and the heads were the first and second chairman. In addition to that, there was a membership secretary, the chief of propaganda, and several committee members.

> Murphy has the wrong dates. The Stackpole translation, RH-translation, and Ford translation all have the correct dates. Murphy also dropped a part of the sentence about the by-laws or rules.
> It appears that many of Murphy's numbers were often off by one year when they were in a range of dates but he was correct on individual dates. This is especially odd because the numbers were the same in German and English.

INACCURATE

Murphy translation: But it seems to me a matter of absolute necessity to take a decisive stand against that view, to make no concessions whatsoever to this fear of responsibility, even though it takes some time before we can put fully into effect this concept of duty and ability in leadership, which will finally bring forward leaders who have the requisite abilities to occupy the chief posts.

CORRECT

Ford translation: Even if it takes a long time before this goal is realized, I will ultimately create an understanding among the members that leaves no doubt about the duty and ability of a leader, and this will allow only those who are truly called-forth and chosen to become leaders.

> This is an example of how Murphy translated words but missed meaning.
> Look closely at the very last line of the Ford translation. It references "*called-forth and chosen*" which ties in to a previous description where Hitler described leaders. Murphy missed this tie-in to a previous passage and translated in a general way, thus losing this element of Hitler's style. In the previous reference Hitler said it was of great importance that a leader *both called and*

MEIN KAMPF

chosen and explained the meaning of this in depth. That tie-in was lost here but it has been revived in the Ford translation.

INACCURATE

Reynal-Hitchcock translation: He is subordinate only to the first chairman, who has to take care of the co-operation of all of them, or, respectively, by selecting the persons and by issuing general principles, has to bring about this collaboration in person.

Murphy translation: He is subordinate only to the chairman, whose duty is to supervise the general collaboration, selecting the personnel and giving general directions for the co-ordination of the common work.

CORRECT

Ford translation: He is accountable to the first chairman, who must make sure that all members cooperate, or he must establish cooperation by choosing men who can work together and by establishing general guiding principles.

> The passage actually talks about cooperation or collaboration as shown in the Ford translation, yet Murphy's translation misses the point and generalizes the passage which alters the guidelines set down for the chairman by effectively removing them. The chairman's duty is not to supervise the general collaboration, but to put men together who can collaborate. That was the intent of the original German passage which is lost in Murphy's translation.

INACCURATE

Murphy translation: In the old Sterneckerbräu im Tal, there was a small room with arched roof, which in earlier times was used as a sort of festive tavern where the Bavarian Counsellors of the Holy Roman Empire foregathered....This panelling had been specially put up for the Imperial Counsellors. The place began to look more like a grotto than an office.

Reynal-Hitchcock translation: In the former Sterneckerbrau in the Tal there was a small, vault-like room which in times past had served as some kind of drinking room for the Reichs-councillors of Bavaria.

147

MEIN KAMPF

CORRECT

Ford translation: In the former Sterneckerbräu Valley Inn Beer Hall(in Munich), there was a small, room with a raised ceiling that had previously...Now, the room really seemed more like a vault than an office.

The Murphy description says arched but the original German said the room had a raised ceiling, not arched. The RH translation calls the room vault-like. The RH translators were possibly confused because later Hitler does call it a vault, yet that is not the meaning of this line. The original German does not say it was arched or a vault.

This kind of attention to translation detail is important to avoid losing larger meanings. Sometimes small details can suddenly transform a sentence from logical subject-verb with little meaning into a meaningful sentence that expresses a complex idea. Small details may also be referenced later. This is a simple example showing where details in the Ford translation were decoded for the first time by carefully investigating each word from multiple original German sources until the true meaning was unlocked and by locating photographs of the actual room being described to verify the accuracy.

Murphy again missed vault and made it into grotto(a small cave) later in the paragraph which is also incorrect, the word was originally vault in the later reference.

Wölbung is German for curvature and is what Vault in English would be translated into.

English *cellar* is *Keller* in German and *Cave* is *Höhle* so none of these fit.

The actual German word used was *gewölbeartiger* and it says *...a small gewölbeartiger area...*

this word translates to vault-like but that is not the meaning. In German, "Gewölbeartig" refers to an arched/raised ceiling, it has nothing to do with a security vault, a cave or a cellar. The room being described did in fact have a RAISED ceiling, not arched. The Ford translation says raised-ceiling to avoid any confusion.

148

MEIN KAMPF

INACCURATE

Murphy translation: In December 1920, we acquired the VÖLKISCHER BEOBACHTER. This newspaper which, as its name implies, championed the claims of the people, was now to become the organ of the German National Socialist Labour Party.
Reynal-Hitchcock translation: It had a certain real value after the War because it was the only Right radical newspaper in Munich with ...., presented folkish concerns, was now to be turned into the organ of the N.S.G.W.P.

CORRECT

Ford translation: We stayed there until November, 1923. Earlier, in December, 1920, we had acquired the newspaper Völkischer Beobachter(the Race Watcher). Its name alone advocated racial ideas and this paper was to be transformed into a vital part of the N.S.D.A.P.

> Murphy translates the passage as "the people" and the RH-translation says folkish, but the actual term, or the subject Hitler was talking about, was **race** which is the name of the newspaper(Race Watcher as previously covered). Both Reynal and Murphy used 'nicer' terms than the real word that was in the original German.
>
> As far as "nice" terms go, you have to realize that "völkisch" in itself is a euphemistic term. "Racial" is the closest translation for "völkisch" as used by the Nazi Party but may have a more negative connotation than the somewhat innocent-sounding German equivalent.
> "Racial" is similar to the German "rassisch", but this more negatively charged word seems to have been generally avoided by Hitler.
>
> The first text used "Völkische Beobachter" which is the plural ("Race Observers") whereas "Völkischer Beobachter" is singular ("Race Observer").

149

MEIN KAMPF

INACCURATE

Murphy translation: The current business administration of the movement could not be regularly attended to except we had a salaried official. But that was then very difficult for us...and at the same time would be ready to meet the manifold demands which the movement would make on his time and energy.

CORRECT

Ford translation: We needed a fulltime, paid party official to manage our business affairs. This was difficult for us back then. ...The movement had very few members at this time which made it tricky to find a suitable man among them who could meet all of the movement's demands while requiring very little compensation for himself.

> Murphy's translation is extremely hard to follow and is unnecessarily complex especially when compared to the Ford translation. This is why people thought *Mein Kampf* was hard to read in past translations. The problem was not the original German but the translations.

INACCURATE

Reynal-Hitchcock translation: It is the everlasting merit of this first business manager of the party, who as a business man was really widely trained, that he brought order and cleanliness into the party affairs. Since then they have remained models and could never be reached, let alone surpassed, by any of the subdivisions of the movement. As always in life, superior efficiency is not infrequently the cause for envy and jealousy.

Murphy translation: It is to the inestimable credit of this first business manager of the party, whose commercial knowledge is extensive and profound, that he brought order and probity into the various offices of the party. Since that time these have remained exemplary and cannot be equalled or excelled in this by any other branches of the movement. But, as often happens in life, great ability provokes envy and disfavour. That had also to be expected in this case and borne patiently.

CORRECT

Ford translation: The infinite value of our first business manager, who had a strong business knowledge, brought order and integrity into the departments of the Party. This established a method of operation

MEIN KAMPF

that was unequaled and certainly could not be surpassed by any of the movement's subdivisions. As frequently happens in life, success often causes envy and ill-will. The same had to be expected in this case and it was tolerated with patience.

> The RH-translation translated as *cleanliness*, but it should have been *integrity*, Murphy called it *probity* which was correct but incomprehensible without a dictionary.
> The RH translation says the model could not be reached by sub divisions. That is not the intent of the passage, it should say "*could not be equaled or surpassed*" as shown in the Ford translation. In the very next RH sentence it says "*envy and jealousy*" but those are the same thing, jealous means envious, and envy means jealousy.
> The RH translation of *everlasting* is also inaccurate. The meaning should have been "ongoing" or "endless" which is best said by "infinite". Murphy used *inestimable* in the same place but this too is inaccurate when compared to the true meaning of the original. Here, the Ford translation is correct.

INACCURATE

Murphy translation: Naturally their noble aim and ideal were always the formation of a committee which could pretend to be an organ of control in order to be able to sniff as experts into the regular work done by others.

Reynal-Hitchcock translation: Their most ideal and their highest aim was for the most part the formation of a committee which, as the controlling organ, had to put its expert nose into the orderly work of the others.

CORRECT

Ford translation: Their greatest goal was achieved when they appointed a sub-committee which would have to poke its nose expertly into the work of others and control everything.

> This is an example of a subtle difference in wording which can change the meaning of a sentence. The true meaning is shown by Ford translation where it says the committee will "*poke its nose expertly into*". That means the committee members are experts at poking their nose in other people's business. Reynal and Murphy both miss this subtlety. Reynal's translation seems to say the

MEIN KAMPF

committee was composed of experts who poked their nose into the work of others. Murphy was closer when he said they sniffed as if they were experts, but that is not what Hitler said. The Ford translation is correct.

.

INACCURATE

Murphy translation: Not in word only, but they proved it by the steady and honest and conscientious work which they performed in the service of the new movement. Naturally a well qualified party member was preferred to another who had equal qualifications but did not belong to the party. The rigid determination with which our new business chief applied these principles and gradually put them into force, despite all misunderstandings, turned out to be of great advantage to the movement.

CORRECT

Ford translation: Not only were they loyal in what they said, but they proved it by doing conscientious, good, and honest work in the service of the new movement. It goes without saying that the well-qualified members of the Party were preferred to non-members of the party who were equally well-qualified, but nobody was hired on the basis of his membership in the Party alone. The determined manner in which the new business manager stood for these principles and gradually carried them out in spite of all resistance proved later to be a great advantage to the movement.

> Murphy dropped the entire sentence about *the movement not hiring exclusively party members, but hiring those best qualified.* This is another example of errors from missed lines. Murphy's final translation is also noticeably shorter than other translations in terms of words and pages. Murphy translated *misunderstandings* when it should have been *obstacles* from employees or better stated as *resistance* which is the word used in the Ford translation.

MEIN KAMPF

Original German: Gewerkschaftsbewegung die Befriedigung ihrer Lebensbedürfnisse, zugleich aber auch eine Erziehung er-hält, wird dadurch eine außerordentliche Stärkung seiner gesamten Widerstandskraft im Daseinskampf erlangen.

INACCURATE

Murphy translation: For when the great masses of a nation see their vital needs satisfied through a just trade unionist movement the stamina of the whole nation in its struggle for existence will be enormously reinforced thereby.

Reynal-Hitchcock translation: For a people whose great masses receive the satisfaction of their vital needs by a correct union movement, but at the same time also an education, will thereby experience an extraordinary strengthening of its entire resistibility in the struggle for life.

CORRECT

Ford translation: When the people receive the necessities of life as a result of their trade-union movement, and the people are also properly educated about the goals of the movement, they will be greatly strengthened and the entire nation's powers of resistance in the struggle for existence will be increased.

Murphy dropped the *education* line. It was a complex line and unclear so he dropped it instead of translating it. The RH-translation kept the line, but in RH's version it makes no sense because it is unclear what education it is talking about. The original German is unclear so simple word substitution does not work to translate this passage. Fortunately, Hitler had a habit of introducing an idea and explaining it, then explaining it again. The following paragraphs made the meaning clear which led to the corrected version of this sentence in the Ford translation.

MEIN KAMPF

Original German: Die Gewerkschaften sind vor allem notwendig als Bau-steine des künftigen Wirtschaftsparlaments beziehungs- weise der Ständekammern.

INACCURATE

> **Reynal-Hitchcock translation:** The trade unions are above all necessary as the building stones of the future economic parliaments, that is, the estate chambers.
>
> **Murphy translation:** Before everything else, the trades unions are necessary as building stones for the future economic parliament, which will be made up of chambers representing the various professions and occupations.

CORRECT

> **Ford translation:** The trade-unions are indispensable since they are the building blocks for the future council of economics and they will be the equivalent of our current parliamentary groups.

> The RH-translation says "*estate chambers*" which has no meaning to English readers. The actual translation should be *chambers of parliament*. The word *chambers* was not used in the Ford translation because it can be confusing in English and instead the meaning was spelled out as "groups". Murphy says "*professions and occupations*" which is not the meaning of Ständekammern. Ständekammern were chambers of parliament, generally divided into three groups: Clergy, nobility and bourgeoisie. The Bavarian Senate, from 1946 to 1999, was also called a "Ständekammer" or second chamber of parliament / representation of the people. Here the first definition is the intent of the last word in the German sentence.

INACCURATE

> **Murphy translation:** I always demanded that, just as in private life so also in the movement, one should not tire of seeking until the best and honestest and manifestly the most competent person could be found for the position of leader or administrator in each section of the movement.
>
> **Reynal-Hitchcock translation:** As early as in those days I made the demand that, as everywhere in private life, also in the movement, the individual sections should search...

MEIN KAMPF

CORRECT

Ford translation: Even in those days, just as it is done in private business, I always demanded that we continue searching until the most clearly capable and honest person was found to act as an official, administrator, or leader for the movement.

Both old translations used "*private life*" but the original German meant "*private sector business*" as shown by the Ford translation. Murphy's use of *honestest* is quite unusual even for him.

Original German: Das hohe Maß persönlicher Freiheit, das ihnen in ihrem Wirken dabei zugebilligt wird, ist durch die Tatsache zu erklären, daß er-fahrungsgemäß die Leistungsfähigkeit des einzelnen durch weitgehende Freiheitsgewährung mehr gesteigert wird als durch Zwang von oben, und es weiter geeignet ist zu verhindern, daß der natürliche Ausleseprozeß, der den Tüch-tigsten, Fähigsten und Fleißigsten befördern soll, etwa unterbunden wird.

The literal and unpolished translation of the Original German: The high degree of personal freedom, to them in their work is allowed, is to explain the fact that it fahrungsgemäß the performance of individual freedom by granting increased more than by coercion from above, and it is more likely to prevent that the natural selection process, the Tüch important, skills and industrious carry such is blocked.

INACCURATE

Reynal-Hitchcock translation: The great measure of personal freedom which is hereby granted to them in their activity can be explained by the fact that, according to experience, the efficiency of the individual is increased more by a far-reaching granting of freedom than by compulsion from above, and it must
further prevent the process of natural selection, which is to promote the most efficient, the most able, and the most industrious, from being cut short.

CORRECT

Ford translation: They are granted a high degree of personal liberty in their work because experience has shown that when a man is given extensive freedom, his capacity for work increases greatly, much more than it does by coercion from above. Lack of freedom prevents the natural process of elimination from occurring therefore the system that allows the most capable, able, and diligent people to be promoted is blocked.

MEIN KAMPF

The RH-translation says the purpose of liberty is to "*prevent the process of natural selection*" but this is not what the German version said and not Hitler's belief. The purpose of giving workers freedom is to **encourage** the process of natural selection according to the passage and Hitler's other remarks. In previous sections of *Mein Kampf* Hitler explained at length why the process of natural selection is important so it makes no sense to say here that it is something to be avoided. RH simply misunderstood the translation and thought the word, verhindern or hindern in German, which means PREVENT or HINDER was referring to the natural selection process therefore they translated the passage to mean exactly the opposite of what it was intended to mean.

Hitler used a style here where he stated an idea, then made a positive statement in one sentence and a negative statement in the following sentence to reinforce the idea which is a characteristic style. This style(as well as the meaning) was lost in the older translations but can be clearly seen in the new Ford translation. RH also mistranslated the end of the passage which should be "*blocked*" to their version "*cut short*" which does not make sense in their translation. They were translating words without paying attention to the context and as a result they missed the meaning.

INACCURATE

Murphy translation: For the National Socialist Trades Union, therefore, the strike is a means that may, and indeed must, be resorted to as long as there is not a National Socialist State yet.

Reynal-Hitchcock translation: For the National Socialist union, therefore, a strike is a measure which can and must be applied only as long as there exists no National Socialist folkish State.

CORRECT

Ford translation: The National-Socialist trade-union sees the worker's strike as a method that can, and probably must, be used as long as there is no National-Socialist racially orientated state.

Murphy omitted the word *racial* from his translation and Reynal used folkish which is technically correct but is meant more as an ethnic state, not a true folkish state that focuses on folklore.
In any translation from *Mein Kampf* you can usually substitute populist, racial and ethnic interchangeably. Reynal often used *folkish* as a cleaner way of saying ethnic or racial which are more emotionally charged words. This watering down of 'völkischer'

MEIN KAMPF

into folkish in English weakens much of the meaning of *Mein Kampf*.

INACCURATE

Reynal-Hitchcock translation: But it did not take long before these very foundations disappeared, so that the final result was the same as ours. With the only difference that we had betrayed neither ourselves nor others.

Murphy translation: But it did not take long for these organizations to disappear and the result was what would have happened in our own case. But the difference was that we should have deceived neither ourselves nor those who believed in us.

CORRECT

Ford translation: But it was not long before these organizations disappeared. The end result was exactly as we predicted, but with one difference: in the end, we had not deceived ourselves or anybody else.

> The RH-translation and Murphy's translation both misunderstood the ending and translated it as "*so the final result was the same as ours.*" Murphy said "*...was what would have happened in our own case.*" This does not fit the paragraph. The Ford translation shows that the true meaning was "*...the result was the same as we predicted*".

Original German: ...daß die äußere Freiheit weder vom Himmel noch durch irdische Gewalten als Geschenk gegeben wird, sondern vielmehr nur die Frucht einer inneren Kraftentfaltung zu sein vermag.

INACCURATE

Murphy translation: and must proclaim it, that the freedom of the country in its foreign relations is not a gift that will be bestowed upon us by Heaven or by any earthly Powers, but can only be the fruit of a development of our inner forces.

Reynal-Hitchcock translation: and must always stand for, the view that external freedom will not be handed down as a gift either from heaven or through some earthly power, but rather can be only the fruit of an inner exercise of force.

157

MEIN KAMPF

CORRECT

Ford translation: This is because our movement must, and always has proclaimed that external national freedom is never given as a gift by heavenly or earthly powers, but it can only be the fruit that results from inner strength of the nation.

The Murphy and RH translations both use the word "force", but the original German said *Kraftentfaltung* which technically translates to "power development" or "strength" and here means *strength*. Murphy and Reynal both chose a harsher translation which alters the meaning and the *feel* of the passage.

Original German: Jeder leistet eben seinen Teil; damals opferten wir unser Blut, und heute wetzt diese Gesellschaft ihre Schnäbel.

INACCURATE

Reynal-Hitchcock translation: Everybody does his bit: then we sacrificed our blood, and today this outfit sharpens its beak.
Murphy translation: Each one plays the part that he is best capable of playing in life. In those days we offered our blood. To-day these people are engaged in whetting their tusks.

CORRECT

Ford translation: Everyone does his part. We offered our blood in those days; now these people do nothing but sharpen their beaks.

Murphy changes *"whet their beaks"* which is in the original German to *"whetting their tusks"* which is not what the original said. The ford translation used "sharpen" which is clearer than whetting for the modern English speaker. The Manheim and Stackpole translations were correct in their translations of this passage too.

Original German: ...Marxismus und umgekehrt die stete Festigung der faschistischen Staatsauffassung werden im Laufe der Jahre die italienische Regierung immer mehr

MEIN KAMPF

den In-teressen des italienischen Volkes dienen lassen können, ohne Rücksicht auf das Gezische der jüdischen Welthydra.

CORRECT

> **Ford translation:** ...Italian people more and more without paying any attention to the hissing of the Jewish world hydra.

> When Hitler means hydra he uses the German word Welthydra as in this example where he has referred to the three arms of the Jewish super-state.

Original German: Wie ist es möglich, daß die jüdischen Organe, bis 1918 die getreuen Schildträger des britischen Kampfes gegen das Deutsche Reich, nun auf einmal Treubruch üben und eigene Wege gehen?

INACCURATE

> **Murphy translation:** How can we explain the fact that up to 1918 the Jewish Press championed the policy of the British Government against the German REICH and then suddenly began to take its own way and showed itself disloyal to the Government?
> **Reynal-Hitchcock translation:** How can the organ of a Northcliffe, the loyal shieldbearer of the British struggle against the German Reich, now suddenly practice disloyalty and take its own course?

CORRECT

> **Ford translation:** How is it possible that the newspapers of a Northcliffe, who were the faithful shield-bearers in the British battle against the German Empire, suddenly broke ranks and chose a path of their own? (This idea came from car-maker Henry Ford's newspaper, Dearborn Independent. Northcliffe was a title, Baron Northcliffe, bestowed on Alfred Harmsworth, a newspaper magnate who was also called Lord Northcliffe. He controlled the Times and other papers and was known for influencing propaganda against the Germans in the First World War.)

> > The name Northcliffe appeared in early printings but was omitted from later versions of *Mein Kampf*. RH apparently used an earlier edition and Murphy used a later edition after the name was removed. The Ford translation attempts to include any omitted sections. This German quote is from a later edition which had the

159

MEIN KAMPF

name removed and simply said Jewish Press instead.
The Ford translation is the only one that explained who Northcliffe was or what the reference meant. Readers of the older translations might have known the name in 1920's but no one would recognize it today. Including such historical reference notes makes the entire text more understandable in the Ford translation.

Original German: Jedes Jahr läßt sie mehr zum Kontrollherrn der Arbeitskraft eines Einhundertzwanzig-Millionen-Volkes aufsteigen; nur ganz wenige stehen auch heute noch, zu ihrem Zorne, ganz unabhängig da. In gerissener Geschicklichkeit kneten sie die öffentliche Meinung und formen aus ihr das Instrument eines Kampfes für die eigene Zukunft.

INACCURATE

Murphy translation: Year after year the Jew increases his hold on Labour in a nation of 120 million souls. But a very small section still remains quite independent and is thus the cause of chagrin to the Jew.

CORRECT

Ford translation: Today, there is one great man, Ford, who has preserved his independence and is still irritating the Jews. (*Later editions of Mein Kampf omitted the name Ford, which referred to carmaker Henry Ford. This reference may have been removed at the request of Henry Ford due to social and political pressure he received because of his anti-Semitism; however, it is more likely it was removed by order from Hitler because of a public apology Henry Ford made to the Jews in 1927, which was issued after he was forced to shut down the newspaper, and in court Ford claimed he had no idea what his anti-Semitic newspaper had been publishing.*)

The name of *Ford*, meaning Henry Ford, not the Ford Translation which is not connected, was omitted from later editions of *Mein Kampf* as shown in this German language quote from a later 1943 version. The Ford translation shows the original version with the full quote and explanation. The RH-translation shows the name. Murphy does not show this reference. The Stackpole translation does show it.

160

MEIN KAMPF

Original German: Diese lebenswichtigste Frage dürfte aber wahrscheinlich doch nicht nur einem deutschvölkischen Propheten als tiefstes Geheimnis bekannt sein, sondern vermutlich auch den Lenkern der englischen Geschichte selbst.

INACCURATE

> **Murphy translation:** Now in all likelihood the deep mysteries of this most important problem must have been known not only to the German-National prophets but also to those who had the direction of British history in their hands.

CORRECT

> **Ford translation:** The native German prophet may consider this vital question as the deepest secret known to man, but it is, presumably, known by those who guide the history of England.

> This passage proves how a neutral word like "völkisch" is commonly mistranslated. "*Deutschvölkische Propheten*" are "*German native prophets*". The word „völkisch" could be left out entirely without changing the overall meaning. But, adding it almost proudly stresses their being Germans. You cannot use "populist" in the translation here because it's too negatively charged where the original sentence is not intended to be so intense. Murphy did in fact omit the reference. The Ford translation kept the reference but used native, not populist or race which would be taking the meaning too far.

INACCURATE

> **Murphy translation:** That aspiration is quite as natural as the impulse of the Anglo-Saxon to sit in the seats of rulership all over the earth. And as the Anglo-Saxon chooses his own way of reaching those ends and fights for them with his characteristic weapons, so also does the Jew.
> **Reynal-Hitchcock translation:** i.e., the drive of the Jewish nation to world rule a matter just as natural as the impulse of the Anglo-Saxons on their side to secure dominion over this earth for themselves. And, just as the Anglo-Saxon pursues this course in his way and fights his struggle with his weapons, so also does the Jew.
> **Manheim translation:** With his superficial thinking he has no idea that this is an instinctive process; that is, the striving of the Jewish people for world domination, a process which is just as natural as the urge of the anglo-saxon to seize domination of the earth. And just as the Anglo-Saxon pursues this course in his own way and carries on the fight with

MEIN KAMPF

his own weapons, likewise the Jew.

CORRECT

Ford translation:...a phenomenon that is just as natural as the urge of the Anglo-Saxon to dominate the world. Just as the Anglo-Saxon pursues this course in his own way and fights the battle with his own weapons, so, also, does the Jew. He goes his own way, the way of sneaking into nations and undermining their inner structure.

The older translations missed some important wording and concepts here including *sneaking* and *undermining*. The older translations tried to preserve the original German sentence structure which makes it hard to understand in English.

Original German: Das allein hätte aber doch der Sinn einer Aktion sein können, deren Kosten in die Milliarden gingen, und die wesentlich mithalf, die nationale Währung bis in den Grund hinein zu zerstören.

INACCURATE

Reynal-Hitchcock translation: But that would have been the only sense to an action whose costs ran into millions and which substantially helped level the national defense to its very foundations.

CORRECT

Ford translation: This was the only reason for starting this campaign that cost billions, and which essentially aided in the total devaluation of the national currency. (Cuno's labor strikes contributed to the hyperinflation in Germany making the Mark basically worthless.)

The RH-translation uses *national defense*. The original passage talked about the devaluation of the Mark as a result of strikes which caused hyperinflation. There was nothing in the paragraph about *national defense*.

The literal translation is "... *and helped significantly, to destroy the national currency base.*"
RH misunderstood the German "nationale Währung" which means National Currency and assumed it was talking about defense. They failed to read the rest of the sentence which would have made it clear the passage had nothing to do with

MEIN KAMPF

defense forces.

INACCURATE

Stackpole translation: This hatred against the corrupters of the nation and of the Fatherland was simply bound to explode.

> The Stackpole Translation says *nation and Fatherland.* The nation and Fatherland are basically the same. It should have been translated as *people and Fatherland*. Hitler uses the same word for people and nation. The difference is determined by how it is used. This has confused many *Mein Kampf* translators. The translator here failed to realize the meaning *nation* did not fit the sentence. You can see what the original German actually said in the Ford translation which is correct.

INACCURATE

Reynal-Hitchcock translation: At the end of this second volume I want to bring before the eyes of our adherents and of the crusaders for our doctrine those eighteen heroes to whom I dedicated the first volume of my work,
Murphy translation: I have dedicated the first volume of this book to our eighteen fallen heroes.
Manheim translation: eighteen heroes
Stackpole translation: eighteen heroes

CORRECT

Ford translation: eighteen heroes
   Ford Translation footnote: (*In the final dedication, Hitler says 18 heroes, however only 16 were listed in the Volume 1 Dedication, and only 16 party members were killed in the Putsch. It is interesting that such an error was overlooked or even made. Hitler was likely thinking of the original 16 plus the following deaths of Pöhner and Eckart.*)

> This is a most unusual error which is in the original German. RH has a note about the eighteen which reads: "*The 'eighteen heroes' have since come into their own. Annual ceremonies honor them, and their names must be conned by rote in German schools.*" Apparently RH did not notice that there were in fact only 16 names listed. Neither Murphy nor Stackpole included

163

a note about the discrepancy yet they both listed the correct 16 names in the start of Volume 1.
This was confirmed in the German language edition and it was an error in the original Volume 2 German printing. .
The later printing of 1943 German language editions were corrected to say sixteen. Here, Hitler was likely thinking of two additional Putch members who died later for a total of 18.

Original German: Damals haben diese Kreise die Politik ihrer verräterischen Dynastie unterstützt und sich einen Pfifferling um Südtirol noch um sonst etwas gekümmert.

INACCURATE

Reynal-Hitchcock translation: It is charming, moreover, to observe particularly how the Viennese legitimist circles punctiliously bristle their present labor of the reconquest of the South Tyrol....In those days these circles supported the policy of their treasonable dynasty and did not give a fig about the South Tyrol or anything else.

Murphy translation: It is particularly interesting to note to-day how legitimist circles in Vienna preen themselves on their work for the restoration of South Tyrol. Seven years ago their august and illustrious Dynasty helped, by an act of perjury and treason, to make it possible for the victorious world-coalition to take away South Tyrol. At that time these circles supported the perfidious policy adopted by their Dynasty and did not trouble themselves in the least about the fate of South Tyrol or any other province.

The RH-translation inserts "give a fig" but that wording does not appear in the original German.

Original German: Besonders köstlich ist es noch, dabei zu sehen, wie den Wiener Legitimistenkreisen bei ihrer heutigen Wiedereroberungsarbeit von Südtirol der Kamm förmlich anschwillt.

INACCURATE

Manheim translation: It is especially delightful, moreover, to see how Viennese legitimist circles literally bristle with their present activity for regaining the South Tyrol.
...At that time these circles supported the policy of their treacherous dynasty, and didn't care a damn about the South Tyrol or anything else.

MEIN KAMPF

CORRECT

Ford Translation: It is pleasing to watch those in Vienna, who support the Monarchy system, when their comb swells up to express their outrage in their efforts to regain South Tyrol. Seven years ago, however, the noble and illustrious dynasty, the Royal House of evil—with the lying deceit that they are so proud of—is the very one that helped the world coalition take, among other things, South Tyrol. In those days, these same men were happy to support the policy of their treacherous Monarchy and did not care a bit about South Tyrol or anything else.

> The original German uses a reference to "comb swells" meaning they become angry or bristle up, but this reference is dropped in all older translations except the Ford translation where the original German expression is kept because it fits better than a meaning-substitution word.
> Hitler did not use the word *damn* which is added by Manheim in his translation. Manheim often inserted unnecessary words like "moreover" in the example here.

Original German: Natürlich, heute ist es einfacher, den Kampf für diese Gebiete aufzuneh- men, wird doch dieser jetzt nur mit „geistigen" Waffen aus-gefochten, und es ist doch immerhin leichter, sich in einer „Protestversammlung" die Kehle heiser zu reden – aus innerer erhabener Entrüstung heraus – und in einem Zeitungsartikel die Finger wund zu schmieren, als etwa während der Besetzung des Ruhrgebietes, sagen wir, Brük-ken in die Luft zu jagen.

INACCURATE

> **Murphy translation:** Anyhow, it is easier to join in a 'meeting of protestation' and talk yourself hoarse in giving vent to the noble indignation that fills your breast, or stain your finger with the writing of a newspaper article, than to blow up a bridge, for instance, during the occupation of the Ruhr.
> **Reynal-Hitchcock translation:** ...from some magnificent inner indignation and to get calloused fingers writing newspaper articles than, say, to blow up bridges, tap wires, and the like during the occupation of the Ruhr region.
> **Stackpole translation:** due to righteous indignation-and to cripple one's hands in writing an article for a paper than, for instance, to blow up bridges during the occupation of the Ruhr territory.
> **Manheim translation:** ..from noble, heartfelt indignation - and wear your fingers to the bone writing a newspaper article than, say, to blow up bridges during the occupation of the Ruhr.

165

MEIN KAMPF

CORRECT

Ford translation: It is much easier to talk oneself hoarse in a "protest meeting" expressing righteous anger or to get a sore finger writing newspaper articles than it is to blow up bridges during the occupation of the Ruhr territory. (This is a reference to the saboteurs in the Ruhr after the First World War who blew up railroad tracks etc. after the French took control of the region.)

The German version does not mean *lubricated fingers* (the German-English dictionary definition), or stained fingers as stated by Murphy, or callused as said by RH, or crippled as in Stackpole, and there is nothing in the passage about wearing to the bone. It definitely means *sore fingers*. The sentence is a bit ambiguous. It either talks about excoriating/chafing one's finger while flicking through/pointing something out in a newspaper article or while writing a newspaper article. The German sentence merely states "in einem Zeitungsartikel" and does not contain a verb to clarify the meaning. In context and when spoken with inflection, the meaning is clearer. In written form it loses those elements. The older translations had trouble with the missing verb so took a good guess. Any of the older translations get the point across, but the Ford translation is the most true to the original German meaning for the entire passage.

Also note that the RH translation added "tap wires", but there is no reference in the original German about tapping phone lines or anything to do with wires.

Original German: Jawohl, so liegen die Dinge, meine tapferen Herren Wortprotestler!

INACCURATE

Reynal-Hitchcock translation: Yes, indeed, my brave protestants of the word, that is the way matters really stand !
Murphy translation: And so the matter stands, my brave gentlemen, who make your protests only with words.
Manheim translation: Yes, my brave lip-service protesters, that is how things stand!
Stackpole translation: Yes, my dear gentlemen of word-protests, this is the situation !

CORRECT

Ford translation: Yes sir, my "courageous" Mr. Word-protester, this is

MEIN KAMPF

how things are!

Note how Murphy omitted the "Yes sir" completely. None of the older translations translated Jawohl correctly which made Hitler's words formalized and stiff. They also missed the meaning of the last line. It was not saying *"this is how the situation stands"*. Remember, Hitler was a speaker and used inflection to convey meaning which is lost in writing. The comment was directed at those who protest-with-words and Hitler was telling them that they have been caught, he sees the situation they created, the cat is out of the bag so to speak. He is not merely saying "this is how it is" even though that is the literal translation. Only the Ford translation conveys the actual meaning of the passage.

The original German said *Herren Wortprotestler!* where Herr means Mr. or *men* and Wortprotesteler is clear even to an English speaker, it means word-protester so Hitler was calling those men Mr. Word-protesters. It could also be interpreted as *men word protesters,* but that lacks his intent and is awkward in English. He called them *courageous* in a sarcastic jab, meaning they were actually cowards, but this style was completely lost in all of the older translations. Fortunately, it has been re-discovered in the Ford translation. Word-protester is another made-up word which is common for Hitler's style.

INACCURATE

Reynal-Hitchcock translation: While we devour each other in religious wrangles, the rest of the world is shared.
Murphy translation: While we were exhausting our energies in religious wars the others were acquiring their share of the world.
Stackpole translation: While we devastated ourselves in religious controversies, the rest of the world was parcelled.

CORRECT

Ford translation: While we tore each other apart in religious squabbles, the rest of the world was divided up by the Jew.

Note that the only older translation that understood any part of the passage was Murphy's. None of the older translations appear to have understood the passage was about the Jews and instead calls them "the others" or does not mention them at all. Only the Ford

167

MEIN KAMPF

translation is correct and understandable.

INACCURATE

Reynal-Hitchcock translation: But whoever, from within its own ranks, takes the National Socialist movement away from its proper mission acts most reprehensibly. Whether
Murphy translation: For the National Socialist Movement has set itself to the task of converting those communists. But anyone who goes outside the ranks of his own Movement and tends to turn it away from the fulfilment of its mission is acting in a manner that deserves the severest condemnation.

CORRECT

Ford translation: Converting these Communists is the mission of the National-Socialist movement, however, the person who goes outside of his own movement and deviates from their real mission is a person who's actions are deplorable.

The passage was not referring to the National Socialist Movement as shown in the RH translation. It was saying the National Socialists are *trying to convert communist*, but people who are part of a religion and disregard the goal of their religion by dabbling in the affairs of other religions are terrible people. Reyal missed the meaning and incorrectly made the sentence about the NSDAP. The sentence was not specific to the NSDAP and applied to any movement.

INACCURATE

Reynal-Hitchcock translation: Systematically these black parasites of the nations ravish our innocent young blonde girls...
Murphy translation: Systematically these negroid parasites in our national body corrupt our innocent fair-haired girls and thus destroy something which can no longer be replaced in this world.
Stackpole translation: According to plan these black parasites of nations ravish our inexperienced blond young girls and in so doing destroy...

CORRECT

Ford translation: According to their plan, these negroid parasites of nations rape our innocent blond young girls and destroy something in this world that can never be replaced.

MEIN KAMPF

The word used by the Stackpole translation and RH translation is *ravish*, Murphy uses *corrupt*, however neither is accurate. There is not an exact English equivalent. There is also no German word for ravish, but the meaning of the sentence is *rape*. Although it is not meant, not exclusively anyway, in the violent sense, this is the meaning of the passage. There is no lighter word for rape in the English language that distinguishes forcible and non-forcible rape. Also note that negroid was translated by Reynal and Stackpole as *black*. However, in this usage negroid was not referring to any black race but it meant corruption or the corrupt or impure in Hitler's sense. To ham-fistedly translate it to *black* strips away the original meaning.

Original German: Man muß damals wirklich das Leuchten dieser bürgerlichen parteipoliti-schen Schimmelkulturen angesichts einer solchen genialen Parole gesehen haben!

INACCURATE

Reynal-Hitchcock translation: In those days the glow of these putrid bourgeois party hacks about the genius of such a slogan was really something to see!
Murphy translation: One should have seen how the countenances of these party politicians beamed with the light of their moth-eaten bourgeois culture when the great genius spoke the word of revelation to them.
Stackpole translation: One must really have seen the glowing of these bourgeois party-political mould cultures in response to such an inspired slogan!
Manheim translation: The way these moldy political party cheeses glowed at the sound of such a brilliant slogan was something to behold!

CORRECT

Ford translation: You should have seen how these moldy privileged-class party-politicians lit up in response to such an inspired slogan!

"Schimmelkultur(en)" means "mildew" or "mold". Murphy translated it as moth-eaten, but it has nothing to do with moths. Stackpole used an unusual British spelling of mold, *mould*, which is unusual considering it was an American translation. Manheim omits the bourgeois/privileged-class reference and makes them just a *political-party cheese*, even though *cheese* is not in the original German text and the passage has nothing to do with

169

cheese.

Original German: Die Brücke zum Marxismus war gefunden, und dem nationalen Schwindler war es jetzt ermöglicht, mit „teutscher" Miene und nationalen Phrasen dem internationalen Landesverräter die biedere Hand hinzustrecken.

INACCURATE

Reynal-Hitchcock translation: The bridge to Marxism had been found and the nationalist swindler was now enabled to stretch out a loyal hand to the international traitor, making a 'German' ('teutscher') face and spouting nationalist phrases.
Murphy translation: And thus it became possible for the pseudo-nationalist to ape the German manner and adopt nationalist phraseology in reaching out the ingenuous hand of friendship to the internationalist traitors of their country.
Murphy Nazi edition: Thus it became possible for the pseudonationalist to play the heavy Teuton, to adopt a nationalist pose and at the same time to extend the trusty hand of friendship to the internationalist traitors of his country.
Manheim translation: ......and the national swindler was enabled to put on a Teutonic face and mouth German phrases while holding out a friendly hand to the international traitor.

CORRECT

Ford translation: Now, it was possible for the nationalistic impostor to extend a respectable hand to the international traitor creating a "German-esque" face that was shouting nationalistic phrases.

> The word of importance here in German is *teutscher*. The word *teutsch* means *German,* however this is not the same word because it has *-er* on it. It is the same as in English if we were to say "German-like" or "Germanesque" or in English we might say Tall-ish instead of Tall meaning something-like but not exactly. We could say "he is tall-ish, not tall but not short, closer to tall, tall-ish". Of course there is an even better word in English, simply Germanic. However, that does not necessarily reproduce the original word choice which could have been Germanic if Hitler had wanted to use that word. It was not the word used by Hitler. None of the previous translations understood this fact. They guessed at the

meaning such as in Manheim's case or omitted it completely in Murphy's translation, or simply used the base word and included the German word untranslated leaving it to the reader to figure out what it meant in the case of the Reynal translation.

Here, „teutsch" is very old way of spelling/pronouncing „deutsch". Etymologically, "deutsch" derives from the Germanic word "theoda". The –er ending is merely the necessary inflection of the adjective. "mit teutscher Miene" = "mit deutscher Miene". A proper translation might be "with a Germanic (expression on his) face". The Ford translation correctly expresses the meaning of the entire sentence.

Original German: Er war nicht eigentlich Staatsmann oder Politiker von Beruf und noch viel weniger natürlich von Geburt, sondern er stellte so eine Art politischen Zugeher dar, den man bloß für die Erledigung bestimmter Aufgaben brauchte; sonst war er eigentlich mehr in Geschäften bewandert. Ein Fluch für Deutschlandxxx deshalb, weil dieser politisierende Kauf-

INACCURATE

Reynal-Hitchcock translation: He was not exactly a professional statesman or politician, and, of course, still less one by birth, but he represented a kind of political hack needed solely to execute definite plans;...
Murphy translation: But he belonged to that type of politician who is merely used for liquidating some definite question.
Murphy Nazi Official Version: He was neither a statesman nor a politician by professsion[*sic*], still less a born politician, but he was a kind of political office-boy who was entrusted with odd jobs.
Stackpole translation: but he represented only a sort of political dummy whom one used only for the completion of certain tasks ;

CORRECT

Ford translation: He was not a statesman or politician by profession and he certainly was not one by birth, but he represented a sort of political yes-man that could be used for the completion of certain tasks.

The older translations say "*a kind of political hack..*" or *dummy* or *office-boy* or *liquidating*. The original meaning was not that he was a dummy, or that he was a hack, or that he was a good worker. It meant he would do what he was told, he was a *yes-man*. Office-boy and liquidating are not far off but they are not as precise as they could be.

This is also a good comparison showing the differences between Murphy's official Nazi edition and the final Murphy edition published by Houghton and Mifflin. There are some major differences between the Murphy Nazi and final British editions.

It is difficult to find a good translation for, or even an example of "Zugeher" which is a noun that doesn't exist in German. It's based on the verb "zugehen" ("approach"). Basically, it means that this person can be approached when certain jobs need to be done. He's like a contact person, a go-fer, or in the Ford translation, a yes-man.

Original German: Wie jämmerlich zwergenhaft erscheinen dagegen unsere deutschen Auch-Staatsmänner, und wie muß einen der Ekel würgen, wenn diese Nullen mit ungezogenster Eingebildet-heit sich unterstehen, den tausendmal Größeren zu kritisieren; und wie schmerzhaft ist es, zu denken, daß dies in einem Lande geschieht, das vor kaum einem halben Jahrhundert noch einen Bismarck seinen Führer nennen durfte!

CORRECT

Ford translation: How pitifully small are our German pygmies of statesmen in comparison. How nauseating it is when these disrespectful, conceited zeros dare to criticize the man who is a thousand times greater.

Zero means "zero" or "loser" in German. It does not exactly mean nobody as some older translations used repeatedly. If can mean nobody if the reader understands that the meaning is a person of no significance, and not the meaning of no-person or no one.

Original German: Er selbst ist kein Element der Organisation, sondern ein Ferment der Dekomposition.

INACCURATE

Reynal-Hitchcock translation: Jewry itself is not an organizing element, but a ferment of decomposition.
Murphy translation: He himself is by no means an organizing element, but rather a ferment of decomposition.
Manheim translation: he himself is no element of organization, but a ferment of decomposition.

MEIN KAMPF

CORRECT

Ford translation: The Jew is not an organizer, but an enzyme of decomposition.

> The Ford translation says *enzyme of decomposition* which makes sense. The other translations us the German word *Ferment* as *ferment* which is not as clear or accurate as enzyme. It is the result of the change in language over time.
>
> Ferment does mean a yeast or bacteria, but ferment is generally used as fermented or fermenting, a verb, which makes the meaning to modern readers unclear with *ferment*. Again the original definitions were technically correct when using a German-English dictionary, but the meaning of the overall sentence is confused and unclear. The German word was *Ferment,* however other German words also mean ferment such as gären treiben vergären gären lassen Gärmittel(a noun). The original German word can also mean to-sour to-turn to-ferment or an element that ferments such an enzyme, but in the context of this passage the best meaning is an organism that promotes decay which is an enzyme. "Ferment" is an old word for "enzyme" in German.

Original German: 1. weil die Machtmittel fehlen, um sie aus dem Dunst der Vereinsabende in die Wirklichkeit umzusetzen, und...

INACCURATE

Murphy translation: (1) Because there are no available means of extricating it from the twilight atmosphere of political soirees and transforming it into reality.
Manheim translation: (1) because the instruments of power are lacking to remove it from the vapors of club evenings into reality;

CORRECT

Ford translation: First, because they lack the strength to move their idea from the haze of night clubs into reality and second, …

> The older translations obscure what should be a simple meaning which is expressed in the Ford translation.

173

MEIN KAMPF

Murphy, RH and Manheim did not understand the passage or they would not have used words like *extricating* or *vapors*. They simply did not understand that it was talking about a *night club* which had a smoky or hazy atmosphere and that is why they used the literal translation term *club evenings* instead. This is accurate because it is talking about a club or bar in the evening, out with friends or co-workers. However, in the English language we would say *night club* to mean a club people go to in the evening to talk. A German would not use Vereinsabende to mean nightclub and would say Diskothek or Nachtclub instead. However, we must look at the meaning and not the literal translation. Today we may consider a nightclub as a place of dancing and drinking, but it also means a bar where men gather in the smoke to talk and that is the meaning here. It could have easily been translated as bar, or assembly of people, or club, or evening gathering, but the real meaning was a *smoky night club*. Manheim's translation may be considered correct but "club evenings" in the middle of a confusing sentence does not have any meaning to English speakers. It clearly means evenings at a club, but is that club house, a social club, or what exactly does it mean? The English reader could easily be confused by the word club without more elaboration. The true meaning is men who are in power sitting in a smoky nightclub.

Original German: So sehr also eine aktive Bündnispolitik gebunden ist an die nötige Werteinschätzung unseres Volkes, so sehr ist diese wieder bedingt durch das Bestehen einer Regierungsgewalt, die nicht Handlanger sein will für fremde Staaten, nicht Fronvogt über die eigene Kraft, sondern vielmehr Herold des nationalen Gewissens. Besitzt unser Volk aber eine Staatsleitung, die darin ihre Mission sieht, so werden keine sechs Jahre vergehen und der kühnen außenpolitischen Leitung des Reiches wird ein ebenso kühner Wille eines freiheitsdurstigen Volkes zur Verfügung stehen.

INACCURATE

Reynal-Hitchcock translation: Just as intimately as an active alliance policy is linked to the necessary evaluation of our people, so is this evaluation again conditioned by the existence of a government power which does not seek to be a handyman for foreign States, not a taskmaster curtailing its own power, ...

Murphy translation: In order that our nation may undertake a policy of alliances, it must restore its prestige among other nations, and it must have an authoritative Government that is not a drudge in the service of foreign States and the taskmaster of its own people, but rather the herald of the national will.

Manheim translation: Much, therefore, as an active alliance policy is linked with the necessary evaluation of our people, the latter is equally dependent on the existence of a governmental power which does not want to be a handyman for foreign countries, not a taskmaster over its own strength, but a herald of the national conscience. P 633

CORRECT

Ford translation: A strong alliance policy depends on our nation receiving the necessary amount of respect from other countries. This respect depends on the existence of a powerful government that refuses to be nothing more than a collaborator with foreign states or the caretaker who finds it unpleasant to manage its own strength, but ...

The RH translation, it is often confusing. Many translated passages do not make sense such as this example where it says *"taskmaster curtailing its own power"*. If one is a taskmaster, then he is a boss, a supervisor, a slave-driver over others. If he were a taskmaster over himself then he would drive himself hard to do a good job. The RH passage appears to say a taskmaster voluntarily limits his own power. However, Hitler is talking about the weakness and cowardice of the government so that is not the meaning and neither is the voluntary limiting of one's own power. The reference was to the government being a taskmaster to the people, not to itself. A reader paying attention would become confused when they encountered this sentence in the old translations because it simply makes no sense in the context of the paragraph.

If we look closer we will then see both the RH translation and Murphy's translation had a misunderstanding of Fronvogt or fron-vogt meaning in English an overseer or caretaker. Murphy said *taskmaster of its own people,* but that is not exactly accurate though not completely wrong either. The original said *over its own power,* not *people and taskmaster.* It is inaccurate for Fronvogt and Kraft was the word used which does not mean people, it means force/strength/power/energy/ ability/virtue.

"Fronvogt" means "socage overseer". In the Middle Ages, this person made sure the feudal duties were carried out properly. You can see the best expression in the Ford translation, but compare all of the versions.

Original German: Der zweite Einwand, die große Schwierigkeit der Um-stellung der feindlichen Völker zu freundschaftlich Verbündeten, kann wohl so beantwortet werden:

MEIN KAMPF

INACCURATE

Murphy translation: The third objection referred to the difficulty of changing the ex-enemy nations into friendly allies. That objection may be answered as follows:

Reynal-Hitchcock translation: The second objection, the great difficulty of the transformation of hostile nations into friendly allies, can be well answered thus:

CORRECT

Ford translation: To the second question regarding the great difficulty in changing the previous enemy nations into friendly allies, we offer the following answer:

> Murphy translated the passage as *third*, but the original German indicated it was the *second* objection.
> There were three previous questions asked. Apparently Murphy tried to make a correction, but his correction used the wrong number and contradicts previous passages in his own translation. The German word zweite means second, not third and it is unlikely any German speaker would miss this meaning because the word for third, drittens, is obviously different.
> The questions in the original text were
> 1. anyone willing
> 2. possible to change attitudes of enemy nations towards Germany
> 3. possible over Jewry

Original German: Friedensverträge, deren Forderungen wie Geißelhiebe Völker treffen, schlagen nicht selten den ersten Trommelwirbel für die spätere Erhebung.

INACCURATE

Reynal-Hitchcock translation: Peace treaties whose demands are a scourge to a people not infrequently beat the first drum roll for a coming rebellion.

Murphy translation: Peace treaties which make demands that fall like a whip-lash on the people turn out not infrequently to be the signal of a future revival.

Manheim translation: Peace treaties whose demands are a scourge to the nations not seldom strike the first roll of drums for the uprising to come.

MEIN KAMPF

CORRECT

Ford translation: Peace treaties which strike demands upon the people, like lashes from a whip, frequently turn out to be the first drumbeat signaling an approaching rebellion.

Hitler compared the peace treaties to a scourge of blows and then that image became the first drumbeat of change. This style was lost in the older translations. His order of words and phrases was important here because it established a rhythm which is shown in the Ford translation. This style was simply written out of the older translations.

It's unclear what exactly is meant by "Erhebung". "Einen Vertrag erheben" doesn't make any sense, so "Erhebung" must refer to something else, most probably an outcry or an uprising by the people. Hence, "settlement of accounts" would not be a good translation so it is better stated as "coming rebellion".

Original German: Der Schmied steht wieder am Amboß, hinter dem Pfluge wandelt der Bauer, und in der Studierstube sitzt der Gelehrte,...

INACCURATE

Murphy translation: And the farmer drives his plough. The scientist is in his laboratory.

CORRECT

Ford translation: Again today, millions of men are working industriously and diligently as if no revolution had ever brought destruction. The blacksmith is again standing at his anvil, the farmer is at the plow, and the scholar sits in his study.

Murphy says *scientist in his laboratory* which is not in the original German text. The Ford translation is correct when it says *scholar in his study*. That matches the original German.

177

MEIN KAMPF

Original German: Allein auch in dieser Zeit sind die guten Grundelemente unserem Volke nicht ganz verlorengegangen, sie schlummern nur unerweckt in der Tiefe, und manches Mal konnte man wie Wetterleuchten am schwarzbehangenen Firmament Tugenden aufstrahlen sehen, deren sich das spätere Deutschland als erste Anzeichen einer beginnenden Genesung einst erinnern wird.

INACCURATE

Reynal-Hitchcock translation: In this period, too, however, the sound basic elements of our people have not been wholly lost, they only slumber unawakened in the depths, and sometimes one may see, radiantly shining like summer lightning in a darkling firmament, virtues which a later Germany will some day recall as the first omen of a dawning convalescence.

Murphy translation: They slumber in the depths of the national conscience, and sometimes in the clouded firmament we see certain qualities like shining lights which Germany will one day remember as the first symptoms of a revival.

CORRECT

Ford translation: Those qualities are sleeping underneath the surface and once in a while, like lightning against the dark curtain of night, virtues flare up which the future Germany will someday remember as the first signs of an approaching recovery.

The RH-translation missed the *lightening on a dark sky* reference. The *darkling* word is the one originally in RH and it is a real word which means *in the dark*. Murphy was about the same. The German word schwarzbehangenen is schwarz behangenen or *dark draped* meaning *curtain of night*. "Firmament" refers to the *canopy of sky*, but "curtain of night" is how it would be said in English. This is not a random grouping of words, it is a common saying. Phrases such as "curtain of night" and "flock of geese" ares encountered often in translations.

MEIN KAMPF

Original German: Die Unterdrückungen von seiten unserer Feinde finden nicht mehr das rechtsprechende Lachen von einst, sondern verbitterte und vergrämte Gesichter. Ein großer Wechsel in der Gesinnung hat sich ohne Zweifel vollzogen.

INACCURATE

Murphy translation: The oppression which we suffer from at the hands of our enemies is no longer taken, as it formerly was, as a matter for laughter; but it is resented with bitterness and anger. There can be no doubt that a great change of attitude has taken place.
Reynal-Hitchcock translation: Oppressions from the side of our enemies no longer meet, as once, justifying laughter, but bitter and woe-begone faces.
Manheim translation: The repressions on the part of our enemies no longer meet the same condoning laughter as formerly, but grieved, embittered faces.

CORRECT

Ford translation: The oppression coming from our enemies is no longer met with approving laughter, but now they are met with bitter and worn faces. There is no doubt that a great change in our attitude has taken place.

Murphy drops the reference to faces in his version. Hitler made a two sided remark, one laughter the other bitter faces but Murphy reworded the sentence. The RH translation can be confusing. It seems to say "oppression is no longer met-it justified laughter" which makes the reader ask *does the oppression justify laughter?* Here, justify is the wrong word. The Stackpole Translation said *one-time smile,* but others say *laughter in past times,* the Ford translation says *laughter* which matches the original German.

The actual translation means "laughter". A good translation might be "the approving laughter". No connection is made between the laughter and the faces in the original German. The enemies used to be met with laughter, and now they're met with bitter faces. That was the original meaning.

INACCURATE

Reynal-Hitchcock translation: revolutionary bedbugs, knapsack Spartacists, en gros and en detail.
Murphy translation: Therein lay the country's misfortune; for they were only revolutionary bugs, Spartacists wholesale and retail.

179

MEIN KAMPF

Stackpole translation: but they were, as a whole and singly, nothing but the vermin of revolution, petty Spartacists.

CORRECT

Ford translation: They were nothing more than revolutionary bugs, knapsack Spartacists, one and all.

> This is a phrase which is common in German and in English. It is "one and all" as in "they are scoundrels, one and all". It is a variation of "each and every one" in English. Stackpole understood the meaning but did not get the correct phrase. RH appears to have not understood so they used the original Latin which was quoted by Hitler. Though that is what he said, no modern reader who had not attended a classical school would understand the Latin phrase. Murphy completely missed the meaning calling it "wholesale and retail" which has nothing to do with the passage.

INACCURATE

Reynal-Hitchcock translation: It is ridiculously illogical to kill a fellow who has betrayed a cannon, while next door in the highest offices there sit scoundrels who sold an entire realm, who have two millions of dead on their consciences, who must be made responsible for millions of cripples, but who meanwhile unperturbedly go about carrying on their republican business transactions.
Murphy translation: for the millions maimed in the war and who make a thriving business out of the republican regime without allowing their souls to be disturbed in any way.

CORRECT

Ford translation: It is ridiculous and illogical to kill a fellow who has betrayed the location of an artillery storage facility to the enemy while, nearby in the highest positions of authority, sit zeros who sold out a whole country.(This reference regards executing informers in Germany who revealed arms cache locations to the Allies after the First World War, this is not a reference to betrayal during wartime.) These zeros have the sacrifices of two million dead on their conscience and are responsible for millions of cripples. Yet, at the same time, they remain spiritually calm and carry on their business of running the republic as usual.

> The RH translation omitted the spiritual/soul reference. This may seem minor, however collectively removing references

MEIN KAMPF

like this changes the overall work of *Mein Kampf* into a different book which is not true to Hitler's original story. Removing references about Fate, soul, and other religious suggestions changes the flavor of the text as a whole.

The RH translation is difficult to understand such as where it says, "betray a cannon". It means to betray the location of artillery to the enemy which we can figure out, but it is one of those odd statements that makes the reader double-read before he realizes what is being said. If it were spoken in a speech, it would be clear, but in writing it is not so clear. The Ford translation has an expanded version to make the meaning clear while preserving the original style.

INACCURATE

Reynal-Hitchcock translation: but that some day a German national court will have to sentence and to execute some ten thousand of the organizing and thus responsible criminals of the November treason and of all that is involved in this.

CORRECT

Ford translation: Someday, a German national court of law will have to condemn and execute ten thousand or so of those organizers and criminals who were responsible for the November treason and all the consequences that followed.

The RH-translation missed the meaning in the last part of the sentence. The Ford translation is correct, Murphy was also correct here(not shown).

INACCURATE

Reynal-Hitchcock translation: Not only that these effective attack formations of the Revolution now felt themselves to be betrayed because they were not satisfied and not only that they wanted to continue to battle of their own accord, their unruly rowdyism was only too welcome to the wirepullers of the Revolution.
Murphy translation: But their illimitable racketeering became odious even to the wire-pullers of the Revolution.
Stackpole translation: Not alone because these activistic attack-formations of the Revolution felt themselves deceived because they

181

were not satisfied and on their own initiative wanted to continue the attack, was their uncontrolled brawling desired by those who pulled the strings of the Revolution themselves.

CORRECT

Ford translation: The angry ruffian masses were not alone because these activist attack troops of the Revolution felt they too had been deceived. They were not satisfied with the results of the Revolution and they wanted to continue the attack on their own. Their uncontrolled brawling was becoming unpleasant even for those who pulled the strings of the Revolution

> The RH-translation and Stackpole's translation missed the word *not* which was important to the meaning. They say the puppeteers WANTED the uncontrolled brawling. The Stackpole translation is actually confusing and appears to have a question tacked on the end which implies an incorrect assumption by the translator. Only the Murphy and Ford translations correctly translated the passage with the negative statement by saying the puppeteers did NOT like the brawling. This Stackpole Translation quote is a good example of the problems throughout the Stackpole book. Also the older translations missed the fact that both the lower masses and the militant political parties were angry, not just the political parties, this is corrected in the Ford translation.

INACCURATE

Murphy translation: His first skilled tactics in the struggle with the rest of the animals undoubtedly originated in his management of creatures which possessed special capabilities.
Reynal-Hitchcock translation: His first intelligent measures in the fight with other animals have certainly been, according to their origin, acts of certain particularly able individuals.

CORRECT

Ford translation: Man's first clever steps in the battle to control other animals must surely have been made by members of his civilization who were particularly gifted.

> Murphy thinks *creatures* have special abilities, but this is not accurate and does not fit the paragraph. The RH-translation misses the point of the animals which is to use them for man's own needs. The Ford translation is correct.

MEIN KAMPF

Original German: ...Europas entspricht eben-sosehr der sadistisch-perversen Rachsucht dieses chauvinistischen Erbfeindes unseres Volkes wie der eisig kalten Überlegung des...

INACCURATE

Manheim translation: perverted sadistic thirst for vengeance of this hereditary enemy of our people as is the ice-cold calculation of the Jew thus...
Murphy translation: in the very heart of Europe, is in accord with the sadist and perverse lust for vengeance on the part of the hereditary enemy of our people, just as it suits the purpose
Reynal-Hitchcock translation: ...responds equally to the sadistic perverse vengefulness of this chauvinistic, hereditary enemy of our people, and to the ice-cold plan of the Jews thus

CORRECT

Ford translation: This corruption matches the sadistic perverse vindictiveness of this fanatically-patriotic, arch-enemy of our people, they are just like the icy-cold calculating Jews who uses this method to begin the bastardization process starting from the heart of Europe, and through infection by inferior people, they plan to deprive the white race of the foundations for a sovereign existence.

All of the older translators used the phrase "hereditary enemy". This phrase occurs a number of times (Erbfeindes), but it is more accurate as life-long-enemy, however life-long makes no sense when talking about a country's life-long enemy in English so it could have been more accurately translated as arch-enemy. It could also be translated as *the enemy we have always had* or *the enemy of our forefathers and still our enemy today*. The original meaning of hereditary was that the country was the enemy of our forefathers and we have inherited the enemy and it will be passed on to our descendants. The German word Erbfeindes literally translates to *Hereditary enemy* so the older translations appear to be correct, but when we look at the larger context and understand the meaning we see a different picture. There is a very similar word Er**Z**fiendes which is arch-enemy. Only one letter difference. It is very possible this is an original German editing error because, based on the context and Hitler's previous discussions of France. He would also consider them an arch or mortal enemy. Hitler also dictated the book so it may have simply been misunderstood and written down or typed wrong. Either way of interpreting the passage yields the

183

MEIN KAMPF

same result therefore the Ford translation uses the more likely translation and equally accurate form of arch-enemy. This makes more sense to English readers and they can understand the meaning instantly.

"Hereditary enemy" = "Erbfeind" (so this is correct, at least technically)
"Mortal enemy" = "Todfeind"
"Arch-enemy" = "Erzfeind" (notice the similar spelling, but the meaning is very different!)

INACCURATE

Reynal-Hitchcock translation: One must not allow the differences of the individual races to tear up the greater racial community.
Murphy translation: The differences between the various peoples should not prevent us from recognizing the community of race which unites them on a higher plane.

CORRECT

Ford translation: The differences between individuals must not be allowed to break down the greater racial community that they share.

Both older translations imply that *races should live together in harmony* or that somehow all races are equal. This was not the original intention of the passage(it should have been obvious that was not what Hitler was saying!).
The Ford translation is correct. The passage means *petty differences among communities should not interfere with a common community of Aryans*.

INACCURATE

Murphy translation: There were three events which turned out to be of supreme importance for the subsequent development of the Storm Detachment.

In *Mein Kampf* Hitler makes a list of important events, three events. Murphy lists the first two but fails to enumerate the third. This is in the final pages where his translation became a bit more sloppy.

MEIN KAMPF

INACCURATE

Murphy translation: Already in the school, unfortunately, more value is placed on 'confession and full repentance' and 'contrite renouncement', on the part of little sinners, than on a simple and frank avowal.

Reynal-Hitchcock translation: Unfortunately, even at school one puts more stress upon the 'repenting' confession and the 'contrite abjuration' by the little sinner than upon a frank admission.

CORRECT

Ford translation: Unfortunately, even in school, instructors attach more importance to remorseful-confessions and to the promises "not to do it again," by the little sinner, than they do to an honest admission.

> Both older translations were literal which missed the "*promise not to do it again*" meaning of the sentence shown in the Ford translation.

INACCURATE

Murphy translation: A patient suffering from cancer and who knows that his death is certain if he does not undergo an operation, needs no 51 per cent probability of a cure before facing the operation. And if the operation promises only half of one per cent probability of success a man of courage will risk it and would not whine if it turned out unsuccessful.

Reynal-Hitchcock translation: A person suffering from cancer, whose death is otherwise certain, need not first figure out fifty-one per cent in order to risk an operation. And if the latter promises a cure with only half of a percent probability, a courageous man will risk it, otherwise he should not whimper for his life.

CORRECT

Ford translation: A victim of cancer, whose death is a certainty otherwise, does not need to calculate a fifty-one per cent chance of success in order to risk an operation. Even if this operation offered only a one-half of one per cent chance of success, a courageous man will not hesitate to risk surgery, and if he chooses not to take the risk, he should not whimper for his life.

MEIN KAMPF

The last lines in the Murphy edition indicates the person should not whimper if the operation was unsuccessful, however that is not the meaning of the passage. The passage says he should not whimper for his life if he chooses not to undertake the operation. Hitler's mother died from cancer which he took heavily. It is a recurring theme in his examples. The RH and Ford translations are correct.

INACCURATE

Murphy translation: The first term, Party, kept away all those dreamers who live in the past and all the lovers of bombastic nomenclature, as well as those who went around beating the big drum for the VÖLKISCH idea.
Reynal-Hitchcock translation: This was also the main reason why we first chose the name 'party.' We had reason to hope that through this alone quite a swarm of these folkish sleepwalkers would be scared away.

CORRECT

Ford translation: The word Party scared off the fanatics who live in the past, as well as the big talkers who spout meaningless phrases about the so-called "populist idea". The other part, National Socialist German Workers, freed us from a whole parade of knights of the "intellectual" sword and all the ragged misfits that carry the "intellectual weapon" as a shield to cover their cowardice.

> There was no *big drum* reference in the original German text as shown in Murphy's embellished version. Neither Murphy or RH used the term Populist which was correct here. This term was repeatedly translated as folkish in Reynal's translation which, as previously discussed, is not the best translation. Murphy left it untranslated for some reason.

INACCURATE

Murphy translation: Everything on this earth can be made into something better.
Reynal-Hitchcock translation: Everything in this world can be improved.

MEIN KAMPF

CORRECT

Ford translation: Every negative event in the world can be turned into a positive one.

> The older translations were literal translations, but they lost the actual meaning of the passage. The older translations file to indicate the passage is talking about events and use the general term *everything*. The passage was not saying everything could be improved or made better, but that every bad event can be turned into a positive one as shown in the Ford translation.

INACCURATE

Murphy translation: His astuteness, or rather his utter unscrupulousness, in money affairs enabled him to exact new income from the princes, to squeeze the money out of them and then have it spent as quickly as possible.
Reynal-Hitchcock translation: His versatility, rather his unscrupulousness, in all money matters knows how to extract, even to extort, more and more money from the exploited subjects who tread the path to nothing in shorter and shorter periods of time.

CORRECT

Ford translation: His skillfulness, or rather deceitfulness, in all financial matters succeeds in sweeping, rather horsewhipping, new funds from the robbed subjects. These exploited subjects find themselves driven down the road to poverty faster and faster.

> The Murphy translation misses the meaning of the passage which about being driven to poverty. The passage in RH is unclear. The Ford translation is the best among these.

INACCURATE

Murphy translation: The division created between employer and employees seems not to have extended to all branches of life.

CORRECT

Ford translation: The separation of employer and employee now seemed complete in every field of life.

MEIN KAMPF

The older translation missed a negator which would have nullified the *NOT*. The older translated sentences also do not make sense in context because it does not fit to say *division did not spread*, because the rest of the paragraph was about how it WAS spreading. The corrected Ford translation has the actual meaning.

INACCURATE

Murphy translation: Occasionally his benevolence might be compared to the manure which is not spread over the field merely for the purpose of getting rid of it, but rather with a view to future produce.
Reynal-Hitchcock translation: He knows very well how to manage; indeed, his charity is sometimes actually comparable to the manure which is spread on the field, not out of love for the latter, but out of precaution for one's own benefit later on.

CORRECT

Ford translation: His benevolence can be compared to the manure that a farmer spreads in the field. The farmer does not spread the manure because he loves the field, but in anticipation of future benefits.

Murphy misunderstood the *Love* translation. Murphy did not understand the role of the word LOVE so he skipped it and neither of the other older translations is clear. Neither is accurate when compared to the original German. The new Ford translation shows the correct translation.

INACCURATE

Murphy translation: Yes, indeed, it must tax all their powers to be able to present themselves as 'friends of humanity' to the poor victims whom they have skinned raw.
Reynal-Hitchcock translation: Yes, it is tiresome work to present oneself suddenly again as ' friend of mankind ' to the skinned victims.

CORRECT

Ford translation: Yes, it is hard work to suddenly stand in front of those victims you whipped raw and present yourself as a "friend of humanity"

The original word used in German was a variation of *flayed* which both older translations incorrectly translated as *skinned* but which more accurately meant *severely whipped*. It did not mean skinned.

188

MEIN KAMPF

INACCURATE

Murphy translation: Thus after a little while he began to twist things around, so as to make it appear that it was he who had always been wronged, and vice versa.
Reynal-Hitchcock translation: After a short time he begins even to twist these things in such a way as to make it appear as though so far one had only wronged him, and not vice versa.

CORRECT

Ford translation: Within a very short time, he begins to twist things to make it appear as if, up until now, it was he who had suffered all of the wrongs and not the reverse.

> Murphy missed the word *not* which completely changes the meaning. The RH translation uses the *not* but the rest of the passage is difficult to understand with so many unnecessary clauses mixed together and the *vice versa* is confusing. Only the Ford translation is both understandable and correct.

INACCURATE

Murphy translation: Goethe was certainly no reactionary and no time-server.
Reynal-Hitchcock translation: Now Goethe was, God knows, certainly no reactionary, far less a helot;..

CORRECT

Ford translation: But Goethe, Heaven knows, was no extreme conservative and not against progress and certainly not a blind follower of philosophy.

> The older translations were direct word-for-word translations where the translator did not understand the actual meaning of the passage and left it to the reader to figure out. Here they mistranslated the German into *helot*(which is neither a slave nor a free person) or in Murphy's version a *time-server* which has no meaning. What was truly meant by the translation of helot was a *blind follower* of some set of teachings like philosophy, or a person who blindly follows others without

189

MEIN KAMPF

thinking for himself. It did not mean a person of *servitude* who served ideas or masters but was his own man who made his own decisions.

INACCURATE

Murphy translation: If that were not so then it would have been superfluous to equip the land forces with 42 cm. mortars; for the German 21 cm. mortar could be far superior to any high-angle guns which the French possessed at that time and since the fortresses could probably have been taken by means of 30.5 cm. mortars. The army authorities unfortunately failed to do so.

CORRECT

Ford translation: If superior strength were not of concern then why were the 42 centimeter field artillery adopted in the army? Larger field pieces would have been unnecessary if they were seeking equality, since the existing German 21 centimeter field artillery was far superior to any French artillery existing at that time. Any fortresses would probably have crumbled for the 30.5 centimeter field artillery.

> Murphy says the army failed to use more powerful equipment, but that was not what the original German text said. It was a comparison between the navy's failure to properly equip their ships with larger guns and the army's correct decision to go to larger field artillery.

INACCURATE

Murphy translation: If the graves on the plains of Flanders were to open to-day the bloodstained accusers would arise, hundreds of thousands of our best German youth who were driven into the arms of death by those conscienceless parliamentary ruffians who were either wrongly educated for their task or only half-educated. Those youths, and other millions of the killed and mutilated, were lost to the Fatherland simply and solely in order that a few hundred deceivers of the people might carry out their political manoeuvres and their exactions or even treasonably pursue their doctrinaire theories.

CORRECT

Ford translation: If the graves spread over the Flanders plains were

MEIN KAMPF

to open today, the bloody accusers would rise from them to point the finger of blame at the Reichstag. Hundreds of thousands of the best young Germans, who were sent poorly trained and half prepared into the arms of death by these parliamentary criminals who have no conscience paid dearly. The Fatherland simply lost these poor souls. These and millions of others were crippled and killed; lost to the Fatherland, lost solely to allow a few hundred deceivers and swindlers of the people to carry out their political maneuvers, enforce their excessive demands, or even test their theories of political doctrine, those traitors.

> The reference to *half trained* actually refers to the troops, not the members of parliament as incorrectly shown in the Murphy translation. This is confirmed in the next paragraph where Hitler says that Marxist parties refused to approve proper training for the troops.

CORRECT

Ford translation: Now it would be a mistake to think that the young fellow who goes to the big city is made of sterner stuff than the one who stays home and makes an honest living from the soil. No, quite the contrary.

> Here, Hitler makes a point about the farm boy who goes to the big city not necessarily being made of sterner stuff than the one who stays home, however in the following several sentences, he explains how emigrants going to the new America and to the big cities from the farms are the best. It is an interesting incongruity. It appears Hitler wanted to make one point, but then was distracted when he praised those who do migrate and never actually made the point he set out to make. He was undoubtedly trying to make a point saying that those who stay on the farm(which is what he wanted) were better people, but that was not the result of his argument, even though that is where the introduction line started to lead.

INACCURATE

Murphy translation: But the greatest credit which the army of the old Empire deserves is that, at a time when the person of the individual counted for nothing and the majority was everything, it placed individual personal values above majority values. By insisting on its faith in personality, the army opposed that typically Jewish and democratic apotheosis of the power of numbers.

MEIN KAMPF

CORRECT

Ford translation: We must consider it a great credit to the army of the old Empire that it placed the individual above mob-rule at a time when majorities were everything, and everyone based their beliefs on the mob's conscience. The army's teaching was in direct opposition to the Jewish Democratic idea that one should blindly worship whatever the greatest number of people believed. Instead, the army upheld faith in the personal values of the individual above the collective values of the mob.

> The original Murphy translation expresses the words but not the meaning. Taken on its own, it has no real meaning and is simply confusing. The Ford translation is much easier to understand.

INACCURATE

Murphy translation: For the authority of the State cannot be based on the babbling that goes on in Parliament or in the provincial diets and not upon laws made to protect the State,...

CORRECT

Ford translation: Strength depends on the universal confidence that can be placed in the administration of a commonwealth and not on the babbling in Parliaments or legislative assemblies(Landtags in some German states), or on laws to protect the State, or on court sentences passed to frighten those who boldly deny State authority.

> The original word which Murphy derived *Provincial Diets* from was Lantags which meant the legislative assembly used in some German states. Diet does mean legislative assembly such as those used in Japan or the Roman Empire but the meaning is not used in common English in this way which makes his translation confusing.

Original German: Die Spinne begann, dem Volke langsam das Blut aus den Poren zu saugen.

INACCURATE

Murphy translation: Like leeches, they were slowly sucking the blood from the pores of the national body.

MEIN KAMPF

CORRECT

Ford translation: This spider was slowly beginning to suck the blood from the people.

Murphy, as well as other translators, changed some of Hitler's examples. Here, Murphy translated "*leeches sucking blood*" but this was not the phrase used by Hitler. Hitler actually said *spiders* as shown in the Ford translation and in the original German version. Although spiders do not suck blood, it is important to keep his original wording and not *correct* his work, otherwise it is no longer Hitler's work. This Ford translation makes a serious effort to maintain the exact wording and exact examples and exact idioms without arbitrarily changing them to match the translators feeling about what it *should* say.

Use of derogatory Kike

Original German: Sowie man nur vorsichtig in eine solche Geschwulst hineinschnitt, fand man, wie die Made im faulenden Leibe, oft ganz geblendet vom plötzlichen Lichte, ein Jüdlein.

INACCURATE

Murphy translation: On putting the probing knife carefully to that kind of abscess one immediately discovered, like a maggot in a putrescent body, a little Jew who was often blinded by the sudden light.

Reynal-Hitchcock translation: When carefully cutting open such a growth, one could find a little Jew, blinded by the sudden light, like a maggot in a rotting corpse.

CORRECT

Ford translation: If you carefully punctured this abscess with a knife, like a maggot in a rotten body, who was blinded by the sudden influx of light, you would discover a Kike.

This is an example of the only time Hitler used the derogatory word Jüdlein in *Mein Kampf*. It is the equivalent to Kike in English. Other instances used Judentum Juden or variations which are the equivalent of Jew or Jewish. Hitler also made a point of ending the sentence with this slur which was important to preserve his style. Murphy and Reynal changed the word order substantially. Murphy misunderstood and thought it meant little-

193

MEIN KAMPF

Jew and so did Reynal, however, little Jew would have been kleiner Jude in German.

Pillory Explanation

> **Murphy:** Further, the way in which they pilloried the German enemy as solely responsible for the war--which was a brutal and absolute falsehood--and the way in which they proclaimed his guilt was excellently calculated to reach the masses, realizing that these are always extremist in their feelings.
>
> **Ford translation:** They were equally vivid in their "festival" nailing-down of the German foe, portraying him as the sole guilty party for the outbreak of the War.

In Manheim and Murphy they made the choice to use a variant of pillory. Let's take a closer look at this translation. First, in German, the term is "Festnagelung" - and it is capitalized. Normally, the term means "to nail down" as with people, one "nails down the time to meet" they are going to meet with someone else. In this way, it's used as a verb. However, Hitler used it as a noun, so it is his idiom. Hitler frequently used verbs as nouns and nouns as verbs.

The meaning is closer to a Festival-Nailing-Down of the German people - a play on words in a way. Hinting at a crucifixion which is not outside consideration since Hitler has so many biblical overtones throughout *Mein Kampf*. If he actually meant something similar to a "pillory" he simply would have used the German "Pranger" - but that doesn't have the more verbally interesting German word-play, as the Festival "Nailing-Down".

This Jesus-Crucifixion reference is interesting. Hitler again used the nailing-down reference in this paragraph from the Ford translation(page 205-6):

> "Those who have known this truth about the possibilities of using lies and slander best have always been the Jews. Their whole existence is built up on one great lie: that they are a religious community when they are actually a race, and what a race! As such, one of the greatest minds of humanity(*Arthur Schopenhauer, the German Philosopher*) forever "nailed-down" an eternally-correct and fundamental truth when he called the Jews "The Great Masters of the Lie". Anyone who refuses to see or declines to believe this can never help truth become victorious in the World."

When Hitler says nailing down and is discussing the Jews, it is very derogatory. When he is speaking of the Germanic Race, it is heroic, like Christ on the Cross.

194.

MEIN KAMPF

These were only a small sample of the errors found. We could not possibly document all of them because some pages had 2, 3, 4, even 5 errors per page. I think the point has been made.

You can read or listen to the Ford translation of *Mein Kampf* by visiting www.Mein-Kampf-Audio.com

You can download free PDF ebooks about Mein Kampf and find other documentary videos and audio programs at www.HitlerLibrary.org

You can find the original German language version of Mein Kampf as well as the Ford translation at www.HitlerLibrary.org

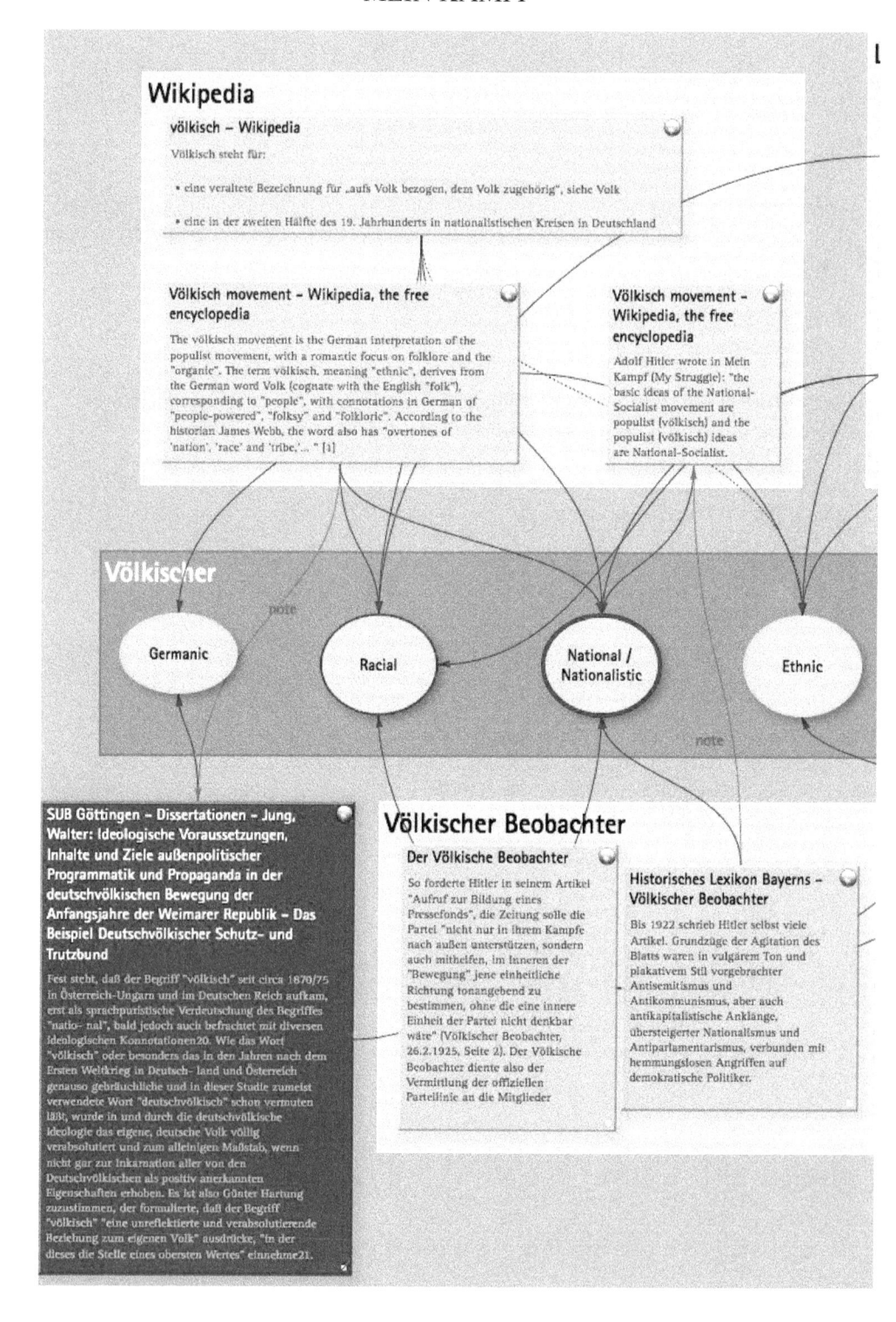

MEIN KAMPF

Wikipedia

völkisch – Wikipedia

Völkisch steht für:

- eine veraltete Bezeichnung für „aufs Volk bezogen, dem Volk zugehörig", siehe Volk
- eine in der zweiten Hälfte des 19. Jahrhunderts in nationalistischen Kreisen in Deutschland

Völkisch movement – Wikipedia, the free encyclopedia

The völkisch movement is the German interpretation of the populist movement, with a romantic focus on folklore and the "organic". The term völkisch, meaning "ethnic", derives from the German word Volk (cognate with the English "folk"), corresponding to "people", with connotations in German of "people-powered", "folksy" and "folkloric". According to the historian James Webb, the word also has "overtones of 'nation', 'race' and 'tribe',..." [1]

Völkisch movement – Wikipedia, the free encyclopedia

Adolf Hitler wrote in Mein Kampf (My Struggle): "the basic ideas of the National-Socialist movement are populist (völkisch) and the populist (völkisch) ideas are National-Socialist.

Völkischer

- Germanic
- Racial
- National / Nationalistic
- Ethnic

SUB Göttingen – Dissertationen – Jung, Walter: Ideologische Voraussetzungen, Inhalte und Ziele außenpolitischer Programmatik und Propaganda in der deutschvölkischen Bewegung der Anfangsjahre der Weimarer Republik – Das Beispiel Deutschvölkischer Schutz- und Trutzbund

Fest steht, daß der Begriff "völkisch" seit circa 1870/75 in Österreich-Ungarn und im Deutschen Reich aufkam, erst als sprachpuristische Verdeutschung des Begriffes "natio- nal", bald jedoch auch befrachtet mit diversen ideologischen Konnotationen20. Wie das Wort "völkisch" oder besonders das in den Jahren nach dem Ersten Weltkrieg in Deutsch- land und Österreich genauso gebräuchliche und in dieser Studie zumeist verwendete Wort "deutschvölkisch" schon vermuten läßt, wurde in und durch die deutschvölkische Ideologie das eigene, deutsche Volk völlig verabsolutiert und zum alleinigen Maßstab, wenn nicht gar zur Inkarnation aller von den Deutschvölkischen als positiv anerkannten Eigenschaften erhoben. Es ist also Günter Hartung zuzustimmen, der formulierte, daß der Begriff "völkisch" "eine unreflektierte und verabsolutierende Beziehung zum eigenen Volk" ausdrücke, "in der dieses die Stelle eines obersten Wertes" einnehme21.

Völkischer Beobachter

Der Völkische Beobachter

So forderte Hitler in seinem Artikel "Aufruf zur Bildung eines Pressefonds", die Zeitung solle die Partei "nicht nur in ihrem Kampfe nach außen unterstützen, sondern auch mithelfen, im Inneren der "Bewegung" jene einheitliche Richtung tonangebend zu bestimmen, ohne die eine innere Einheit der Partei nicht denkbar wäre" (Völkischer Beobachter, 26.2.1925, Seite 2). Der Völkische Beobachter diente also der Vermittlung der offiziellen Parteilinie an die Mitglieder

Historisches Lexikon Bayerns – Völkischer Beobachter

Bis 1922 schrieb Hitler selbst viele Artikel. Grundzüge der Agitation des Blatts waren in vulgärem Ton und plakativem Stil vorgebrachter Antisemitismus und Antikommunismus, aber auch antikapitalistische Anklänge, übersteigerter Nationalismus und Antiparlamentarismus, verbunden mit hemmungslosen Angriffen auf demokratische Politiker.

Lexica / Dictionaries

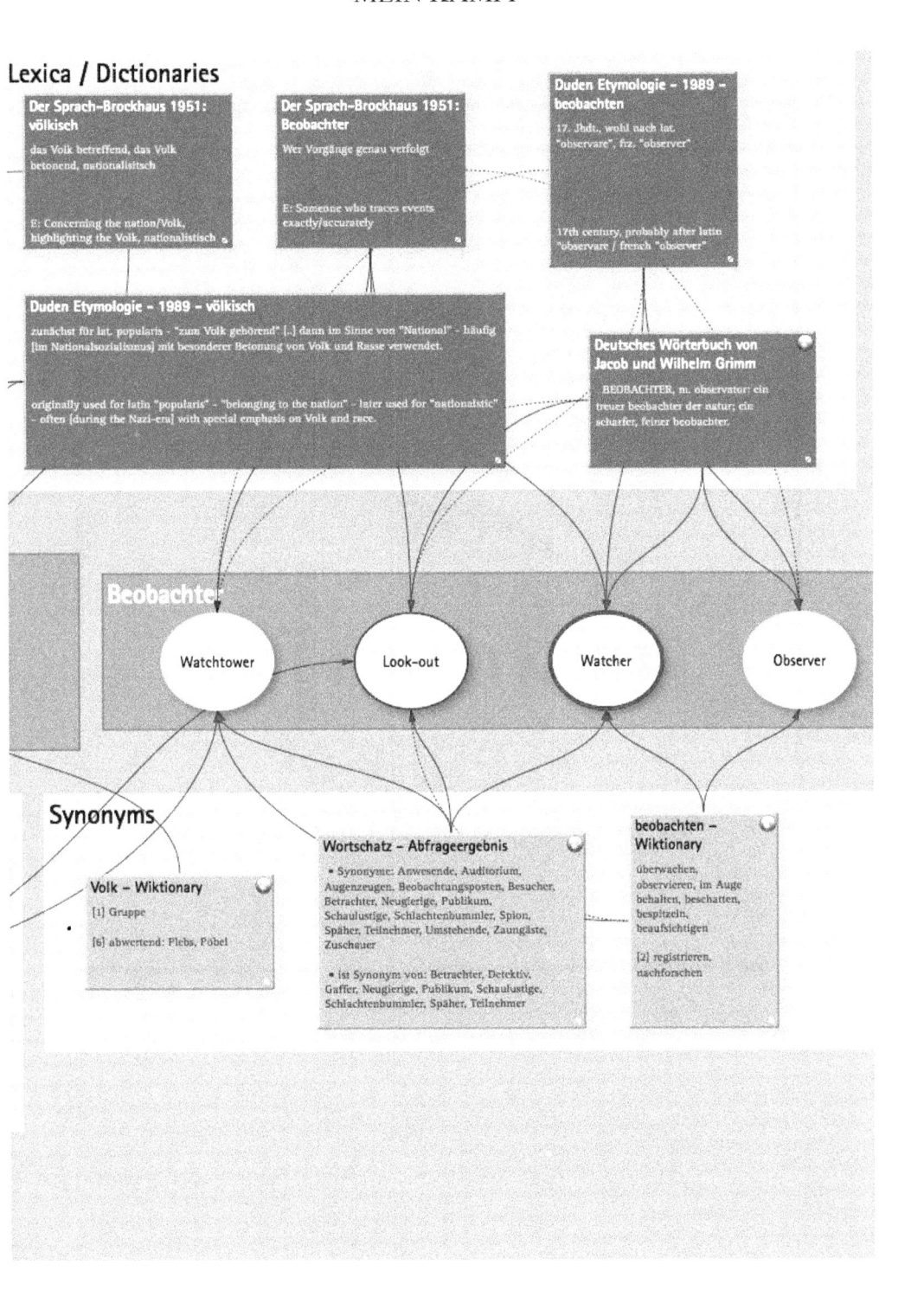

Der Sprach-Brockhaus 1951: völkisch
das Volk betreffend, das Volk betonend, nationalistisch

E: Concerning the nation/Volk, highlighting the Volk, nationalistisch

Der Sprach-Brockhaus 1951: Beobachter
Wer Vorgänge genau verfolgt

E: Someone who traces events exactly/accurately

Duden Etymologie - 1989 - beobachten
17. Jhdt., wohl nach lat. "observare", frz. "observer"

17th century, probably after latin "observare" / french "observer"

Duden Etymologie - 1989 - völkisch
zunächst für lat. popularis - "zum Volk gehörend" [..] dann im Sinne von "National" - häufig [im Nationalsozialismus] mit besonderer Betonung von Volk und Rasse verwendet.

originally used for latin "popularis" - "belonging to the nation" - later used for "nationalistic" - often [during the Nazi-era] with special emphasis on Volk and race.

Deutsches Wörterbuch von Jacob und Wilhelm Grimm
BEOBACHTER, m. observator; ein treuer beobachter der natur; ein scharfer, feiner beobachter.

Beobachter

- Watchtower
- Look-out
- Watcher
- Observer

Synonyms

Volk – Wiktionary
[1] Gruppe
[6] abwertend: Plebs, Pöbel

Wortschatz – Abfrageergebnis
• Synonyme: Anwesende, Auditorium, Augenzeugen, Beobachtungsposten, Besucher, Betrachter, Neugierige, Publikum, Schaulustige, Schlachtenbummler, Spion, Späher, Teilnehmer, Umstehende, Zaungäste, Zuschauer

• ist Synonym von: Betrachter, Detektiv, Gaffer, Neugierige, Publikum, Schaulustige, Schlachtenbummler, Späher, Teilnehmer

beobachten – Wiktionary
überwachen, observieren, im Auge behalten, beschatten, bespitzeln, beaufsichtigen

[2] registrieren, nachforschen

Listen To Mein Kampf

Listen to a free sample at
www.Mein-Kampf-Audio.com

FREE BONUS:

As a special thank-you for purchasing this book, you can download a bonus gift at

http://Bonus.HitlerLibrary.com

This special page contains additional updates and audio information so go there now.